Doing Action Research

in Your Own Organization

D1169765

Doing Action Research

in Your Own Organization

David Coghlan
Teresa Brannick

Sage Publications
London • Thousand Oaks • New Delhi

SAGE Publications Ltd
6 Bonhill Street
London EC2A 4PU

SAGE Publications Inc
2455 Teller Road
Thousand Oaks, California 91320

SAGE Publications India Pvt Ltd
32, M-Block Market
Greater Kailash – 1
New Delhi 110 048

British Library Cataloguing in Publication Data

A catalogue record for this book is available from the British Library

ISBN 0 7619 6886 5
ISBN 0 7619 6887 3 (pbk)

Library of Congress catalog record available

Typeset by M Rules
Printed and bound in Great Britain by Biddles Ltd, www.biddles.co.uk

Contents

About the Authors

DAVID COGHLAN teaches organization development and action research at the School of Business Studies, University of Dublin, Ireland. He has an MSc in management science from the Manchester School of Management (UK), an SM in management from MIT's Sloan School of Management and a PhD from the National University of Ireland. He is co-author of *The Dynamics of Organizational Levels* in the Addison-Wesley OD series (1994) and has edited a special issue of the *Journal of Managerial Psychology* on 'Action Science and Organizational Research' (1995), and the *Organization Development Journal* on 'Organization Development in Voluntary Organizations' (1996) and 'Grandmasters of Organization Development' (1997). He is Associate Editor-International of the *Organization Development Journal* and is on the editorial panel of *Action Research International*. He conducts seminars on the subject of action research and researching your own organization.

TERESA BRANNICK is a lecturer in the business research programme at the Michael Smurfit Graduate School of Business at University College, Dublin, National University of Ireland, Dublin, Ireland. Her undergraduate degree is in mathematics, her masters in sociology and her PhD in marketing research. She has been a practising researcher for over twenty years and has published over thirty research papers in such diverse fields as epidemiology, public policy, industrial relations and marketing. She is editor of *Irish Business and Administrative Research*. Her most recent book is *Business Research Methods: Strategies, Techniques and Sources* (1997, Dublin: Oak Tree Press). She conducts seminars on research methods and on researching your own organization.

Figures

Acknowledgements

We are grateful to those who read unfolding editions of the manuscript text and provided very useful critiques: Gemma Donnelly-Cox, Robbie Gilligan, Evert Gummesson, Pat Joynt, Geoffrey MacKechnie, Eddie McIlduff, Peter Manning, Marc Miller, Peter Reason, Ed Schein, Bill Torbert, David Tuohy, Dan Twomey, Richard Vail and John Van Maanen.

As it was really difficult to find usable materials, we are very grateful to those who supported us in the venture and directed us to valuable sources: Jean Bartunek, Dave Buchanan, Steve Buckley, Andreas Buttimer, Bob Dick, Tony Dromgoole, Victor Friedman, Paul Jeffcut, Rosalie Holian, Bob Krim, Tony McCashin, Joe McDonagh, Liz Mellish, Ry Nielsen, Judy O'Neil, David Quinlan, Joe Raelin, Patrick Riordan, George Roth, John Rowan, Lesley Treleaven and Jack Whitehead.

Successive cohorts of the Masters in Management Practice programme at the Irish Management Institute-University of Dublin and the MBA at the Smurfit Graduate School of Business, University College, Dublin, contributed to refining some of the frameworks as they struggled through their own action research projects. The members of the action research postgraduate seminar at the School of Business Studies at the University of Dublin, Mary Casey, Phil Hanlon, Claus Jacobs, Verena Keane, Phil Killeen, Pat Nolan and Michele Ryan, provided vigorous exploration of the many epistemological and implementation issues in action research. Paula Roberts took our handwritten diagrams and skilfully turned them into graphics. We acknowledge the invaluable help and support of the Sage editorial and production teams, especially Simon Ross, Beth Crockett and Vanessa Harwood.

Preface

Researching your own organization, and more particularly through an action research approach, is a neglected subject in the research literature. When we embarked on the project of this book, we used every opportunity we could to inquire among colleagues, both at home and abroad, at conferences and by e-mail, what they knew has been written on the topic. The typical response was to confirm the paucity of publication on the subject, both theory and case material, and to encourage us to fill this gap. At the same time, everyone we consulted acknowledged that the practice of doing action research in and on your own organization is very common.

What is action research? As the name suggests, action research is an approach to research which aims at both taking action and creating knowledge or theory about that action. The outcomes are both an action and a research outcome, unlike traditional research approaches which aim at creating knowledge only. Action research works through a cyclical process of consciously and deliberately: (a) planning; (b) taking action; (c) evaluating the action, leading to further planning and so on. The second dimension of action research is that it is participative, in that the members of the system which is being studied participate actively in the cyclical process. This contrasts with traditional research where members are objects of the study. Action research is a generic term that covers many forms of action-oriented research, which may be confusing to any prospective researcher. At the same time, the array of approaches indicates diversity in theory and practice among action researchers and provides a wide choice for potential action researchers as to what might be appropriate for their research.

Action research is appropriate when the research topic is an unfolding series of actions over time in a given group, community or organization, and the members wish to study their own action in order to change or improve the working of some aspects of the system, and study the process in order to learn from it. Hence action research is akin to experiential learning (Kolb, 1984) and reflective practice (Schon, 1983).

Doing research in one's own organization means that a member of an organization undertakes an explicit research role in addition to the normal functional role which that member holds in the organization. Therefore, the researcher has to balance the membership role he or she holds and hopes to continue to hold with the additional role of inquiry and research. Doing action research means being engaged in a more rigorous series of diagnosing situations, planning and taking action and evaluating than is perhaps the norm.

There are many issues to be considered for those embarking on research in their own organization or part thereof. From the perspective of individuals who are seeking to do the research in order to achieve academic certification, there are issues pertaining to their academic directors and those pertaining to their organizational superiors. There are issues of gaining access and receiving permission, and building and maintaining support from peers and relevant subsystems within the organization. There are issues of selecting a research question and area for study. In such a case, student-researchers, in effect, take on an additional role to their conventional organizational one, that of active agent of inquiry (Evered and Louis, 1981). This multiple role identity both complicates and focuses the research project. There are issues around how to attain some sense of objectivity and move beyond a personal perspective by testing assumptions and interpretations. There are the uses of appropriate frameworks for viewing and understanding the data. There are questions about how to write up such a research project, give feedback to one's superiors and peers, and disseminate the research to the wider community. Handling interpretations or outcomes which would be perceived negatively by the organization is a particularly sensitive issue.

Who does action research in their own organization? A

common context for such research is one where an individual employee undertakes research as part of an academic programme in order to fulfil requirements for academic certification (Coghlan and McDonagh, 1997; Gosling and Ashton, 1994; Perry and Zuber-Skerritt, 1994). In this instance the individual initiates the research agenda and attempts to negotiate a research project which will meet both her own and the organization's needs. This occurs in full-time and part-time programmes, at doctorate, masters, undergraduate and diploma levels and in business, health care, government, education, social work and third sector organizations. Some research projects may be integrally linked to inquiry into the processes of problem resolution; others may take a broader more comprehensive and diagnostic perspective. At the same time, selection of a research topic from one's own organization is typically attached to an expectation or contract that the research will make a useful contribution to the organization.

READERSHIP

This book is addressed to the reader who is in this dual role of simultaneously holding an organizational functional role which is linked to a career path and ongoing membership of the organization, and a more temporary researcher role for the duration of the research project. While this may imply a distinction between research and ordinary life, we do not intend such a distinction. Our aim is to provide a book which is useful for those who select an action research role in their organization for a temporary period, and for those in academic institutions who supervise such research.

There are many books and articles which address the theory and practice of action research (Argyris et al., 1985; Checkland and Holwell, 1998; Clark, 1972; Eden and Huxham, 1996; Elliot, 1991; Greenwood and Levin, 1998; Gummesson, 2000; Reason and Bradbury, 2000; Schein, 1987; Stringer, 1999; Whyte, 1991). We do not intend retracing what is well presented in these works, particularly with regard to extensive epistemological issues, the history of action research and detailed formats of research interventions. Indeed we recommend that this book be used in conjunction with such works as: Cunningham (1993), Fisher and Torbert (1995), Gummesson (2000), McNiff et al. (1996), Reason and Bradbury (2000) and Stringer (1999).

PLAN OF THE BOOK

The book is divided into two parts. Part I, Foundations, introduces and explores foundational material on action research and doing it in your own organization. Chapter 1 provides a description of action research and introduces its many forms. Chapter 2 describes the action research cycle. Chapter 3 examines how the action researcher can focus on learning in action. Chapter 4 deals with the complexity of doing action research in and on your own organization. We draw on as much case material as we could find and use it to illustrate particular points. Some of the cases we draw on are action research academic dissertations, some are not.

Part II, Implementation, deals with issues of doing action research in your own organization. Chapter 5 explores the important topic of managing organizational politics. Chapter 6 focuses on framing and selecting a project. Chapter 7 outlines the actual process of implementing the project. Chapter 8 introduces some frameworks which can be used for diagnosing organizations and applying theory, and Chapter 9 provides some hints on writing an action research dissertation. We draw on as much case material as we could find, some of which relates to situations of academic accreditation and some which does not.

David Coghlan
Teresa Brannick
Dublin

PART I

FOUNDATIONS

Understanding Action Research

In this chapter we outline the foundations of action research through describing its core tenets and illustrating how it has become a generic term for a wide and even confusing array of related approaches.

Action research is about research and action. In contrast, traditional approaches to research postulate a split between research and action. Scholars in the traditional hypothetico-deductive approach conduct research that meets the criteria of the rigour of normal science but is disconnected from everyday life. In this tradition, research findings and theories can serve as the basis for recommending future action. This split between research and action is, in many respects, a false distinction and not one acknowledged by action research. It is typically based on extreme views of what researchers are and what practitioners are. Gummesson (2000) builds bridges between the two by seeing both groups as 'knowledge workers' whereby each has a different emphasis in relation to theory and practice; one pecks at theory and contributes to practice and the other pecks at practice and contributes to theory. In the context of this historical debate and of the role of practice in organizations, we are focusing on action research as a particular contribution to the subject of researching your own organization.

FOUNDATIONS OF ACTION RESEARCH

Action research has been traditionally defined as an approach to research that is based on a collaborative problem-solving relationship between researcher and client which aims at both solving a problem and generating new knowledge. It developed largely from the work of Kurt Lewin and his associates, and involves a cyclical process of diagnosing a change situation or a problem, planning, gathering data, taking action, and then fact-finding about the results of that action in order to plan and take further action (Dickens and Watkins, 1999; Lewin, 1973). The key idea is that action research uses a scientific approach to study the resolution of important social or organizational issues together with those who experience these issues directly.

Argyris (1993) summarizes four core themes of Lewin's work. First, Lewin integrated theory with practice by framing social science as the study of problems of real life, and he connected all problems to theory. Second, he designed research by framing the whole and then differentiating the parts. Third, he produced constructs which could be used to generalize and understand the individual case, particularly through the researcher as intervenor and his notion that one could only understand something when one tried to change it. Fourth, he was concerned with placing social science at the service of democracy, thereby changing the role of those being studied from subjects to clients so that help, if effective, could improve the quality of life and lead to more valid knowledge. Marrow, Lewin's biographer, states:

> Theory was always an intrinsic part of Lewin's search for understanding, but theory often evolved and became refined as the data unfolded, rather than being systematically detailed in advance. Lewin was led by both data and theory, each feeding the other, each guiding the research process. (Marrow, 1969: 128)

After Lewin's untimely death in 1947, action research became integral to the growth of the theory and practice of organization development (Burke, 1994a; Cunningham, 1993; French and Bell, 1999; Frohman et al., 1976; Golembiewski and Varney, 1999; Rothwell et al., 1995; Weisbord, 1987), and significant for organizational research (Checkland and Holwell, 1998; Eden and Huxham, 1996; Gummesson, 2000; Whyte, 1991), such as commercial organizations (Baskerville and Wood-Harper, 1996; Foster 1972), education (Elliot, 1991; Kemmis and McTaggart,

1988; Quigley and Kuhne, 1997), community work (Stringer, 1999) and health care (Hart and Bond, 1995; Holter and Schwartz-Barcott, 1993; Towell and Harries, 1978; Webb, 1989).

Argyris et al. (1985) summarize Lewin's concept of action research:

1   It involves change experiments on real problems in social systems. It focuses on a particular problem and seeks to provide assistance to the client system.
2   Like social management more generally, it involves iterative cycles of identifying a problem, planning, acting and evaluating.
3   The intended change in an action research project typically involves re-education, a term that refers to changing patterns of thinking and action that are currently well established in individuals and groups. A change intended by change agents is typically at the level of norms and values expressed in action. Effective re-education depends on participation by clients in diagnosis, fact finding and free choice to engage in new kinds of action.
4   It challenges the status quo from a participative perspective, which is congruent with the requirements of effective re-education.
5   It is intended to contribute simultaneously to basic knowledge in social science and to social action in everyday life. High standards for developing theory and empirically testing propositions organized by theory are not be to be sacrificed nor the relation to practice be lost.

Lippitt (1979) distinguishes three different meanings that have been denoted by the term action research which reflect different roles played by the researcher. First, diagnostic research is conducted concerning some ongoing aspect of an action process. In this form of research the researcher gathers the data and presents it to those who are in a position to take some action. The research originates from the researcher's interests and is useful to the organization, partly as a pay-off for allowing access. In Lippitt's view this does not constitute action research. The second meaning of the term action research is connoted by a procedure of collecting data from participants of a system and providing feedback about the findings of the data as an intervention to influence, presumably in a helpful way, the ongoing action process of the system. In this model the researcher may be acting either as a data gatherer solely or in a helping role to the members of the system. The third meaning of action research is defined as a procedure in which the participants of a social system are involved in a data collection process about themselves and they utilize the data they have generated to review the facts about themselves in order to take some form of remedial or developmental action. In this model, the researcher and the researched are working in collaboration. In Lippitt's view this is the purest form of action research.

Cooperrider and Srivastva (1987) criticize how action research has developed to be viewed as a form of problem solving. They challenge what they see as underlying assumptions about the nature of action research, which are based on utilitarian and technical views of organizations as problems to be solved. As an alternative, they propose appreciative inquiry as a form of action research which focuses on building on what is already successful, rather than what is deficient.

For Gummesson (2000: 116) action research is 'the most demanding and far-reaching method of doing case study research'. He integrates the characteristics of action research from several studies and focuses it within a management perspective.

1 Action researchers take action.
2 Action research always involves two goals: solve a problem for the client and contribute to science. This means being a management consultant and an academic researcher at the same time.
3 Action research is interactive; it requires cooperation between the researchers and the client personnel, and continuous adjustment to new information and new events.
4 The understanding developed during an action research project aims at being holistic and recognizing complexity.
5 Action research is applicable to the understanding, planning and implementation of change in business firms and other organizations.

6　It is essential to understand the ethical framework and values and norms within which action research is used in a particular context.

7　Action research can include all types of data gathering methods, but requires the total involvement of the researcher.

8　Constructively applied preunderstanding of the corporate environment and of the conditions of business is essential.

9　Management action research should be conducted in real time, though retrospective action research is also acceptable.

10　The management action research paradigm requires its own quality criteria.

Business consultancy language not withstanding, Gummesson's characteristics apply to the insider action researcher in any organization. The research project unfolds as the cycles of planning, data gathering, taking action, reviewing and further planning and action are enacted. Weisbord (1988) explores the images of taking photographs and making movies in relation to organization development. He describes taking photographs as freezing a moment in time and arranging key factors in a conceptual framework. No photograph takes in the whole of reality; it only takes in what is in the frame. Making movies is an engagement in patterns of activity and relationships by multiple actors who are moving and interacting over a period of time. We find this image of making movies and the insider action researcher as an actor-director pertinent and useful for thinking about doing action research in your own organization.

EXPERIENTIAL PARADIGMS OF ACTION RESEARCH

The term action research is generic and is used to refer to a bewildering array of activities and methods (Miller, 1994). At its core, action research is a research approach which focuses on simultaneous action and research in a participative manner. Within this approach are multiple paradigms or methodologies, each of which has its own distinctive emphasis (Greenwood and Levin, 1998). Some action research methodologies have developed from sociology and focus on how communities as socio-political systems enact change. These approaches tend to focus on structural emancipatory issues, relating to, for example, education, social exclusion and power and control (Fals-Borda and Rahman 1991; Lynch, 1999; Whyte, 1991). Other action research methodologies have their origins in applied behavioural science and have developed in the organizational context (Coch and French, 1948; Foster, 1972; French and Bell, 1999; Schein, 1987).

A significant feature of all action research is that the purpose of research is not simply or even primarily to contribute to the fund of knowledge in a field, or even to develop emancipatory theory, but rather to forge a more direct link between intellectual knowledge/theory and action so that each inquiry contributes directly to the flourishing of human persons and their communities (Heron and Reason, 1997). Action research rejects the separation between thought and action that underlies the pure applied distinction that has traditionally characterized management and social research. These approaches incorporate an action research cycle whereby the intended research outcome is the construction of new knowledge on which new forms of actions can be based.

The various forms and varieties of action research are united by three research attributes or features. First and foremost, these approaches are participatory whereby research subjects are themselves researchers or in a democratic partnership with the researcher. Second, this tradition emphasizes that research itself is a force for, and an agent of, change. Rowan (1981) identified three ways in which research can change the world. It makes a difference to the researcher, to those who come to know about the research, and it makes a difference to whatever or whomever is studied. Here research acts as an agent of change and the researcher is involved in the process of change. Traditional hypothetico-deductive and hermeneutic research approaches address the audience of the community of scholars; and applied practical research addresses an outside audience in reports, recommendations and so on. In contrast, according to Reason and Marshall (1987), all good research communicates with three audiences:

All good research is *for me, for us*, and *for them*: it speaks to three audiences . . . It is *for them* to the extent that it produces some kind of generalizable ideas and outcomes . . . It is *for us* to the extent that it responds to concerns for our praxis, is relevant and timely . . . [for] those who are struggling with problems in their field of action. It is *for me* to the extent that the process and outcomes respond directly to the individual researcher's being-in-the-world. (Reason and Marshall, 1987: 112–113)

Torbert (1998) presents these three audiences as three forms of research, first-person, second- and third-person research.

Action research approaches are radical to the extent that they advocate replacement of existing forms of social organization. Some members of the community or organization being studied become involved in the research process but the process aims at increasing knowledge rather than generating action. These variants challenge normal science in several action-oriented ways. Sharing the power of knowledge production with the researched subverts the normal practice of knowledge and policy development as being the primary domain of researchers and policymakers. Researchers work on the epistemological assumption that the purpose of academic research and discourse is not just to describe, understand and explain the world but also to change it. The issue is not so much the form of the knowledge produced or the methodology employed to gather data/evidence but who decides the research agenda in the first place and who benefits directly from it.

The third and final common theme is that the data/evidence used in the research approach are systematically collected and come from the experience of the research participants. Formal quantitative and qualitative data collection techniques are all appropriate to differing situations (Brooks and Watkins, 1994).

How is action research scientific? Many writers have articulated the epistemological foundations of action research and contrasted them with those of the scientific method associated with positivistic philosophy (Aguinis, 1993; Baskerville and Wood-Harper, 1996; Checkland and Holwell, 1998; Eden and Huxham, 1996; Greenwood and Levin, 1998; Gummesson,

2000; Heron, 1988; Reason and Rowan, 1981; Riordan, 1995; Susman and Evered, 1978). It is not our intention to retrace those arguments here. Readers undertaking an action research project through an academic dissertation will engage in their own review of these philosophical issues. Suffice it to say that action research as a scientific approach does not have to justify itself in comparison to other approaches, but rather is evaluated within its own frame of reference. Questions of reliability, replicability and universality do not pertain to the action research approach. Instead action research poses three questions:

1 What happened? The relating of a good story.
2 How do you make sense of what happened? This involves rigorous reflection on that story.
3 So what? This most challenging question deals with the extrapolation of usable knowledge or theory from the reflection on the story.

In this chapter we will not elaborate on the nuances between the different action research approaches as they are well articulated elsewhere (Brooks and Watkins, 1994; Elden and Chisholm, 1993; Greenwood and Levin, 1998; Raelin, 1997, 1999; Reason, 1994b; Schein, 1995; Whyte, 1991). We will, however, draw on some of these forms with respect to researching your own organization.

Traditional action research
Action research in its traditional sense comes from the work of Kurt Lewin (1973) and involves a collaborative problem-solving relationship between researcher and client aimed at both solving a problem and generating new knowledge. The researcher and client engage in collaborative cycles of planning, taking action and evaluating. This form of action research is central to the theory and practice of organization development (Cunningham, 1993; French and Bell, 1999). It is this form of action research that provides the central theme of this book, and we will draw on Bartunek et al. (1993) as an example of such action research in your own organization.

Participatory action research

Participatory action research (PAR) is associated with the work of William Foote Whyte (1991), the eminent sociologist. PAR is primarily an egalitarian participation by a community to transform some aspects of its situation or structures. It focuses on concerns of power and powerlessness and how the powerless are excluded from decision making, and moves to empowering people to construct and use their own knowledge. Many of the liberation or emancipatory action research approaches are variations on PAR. We will refer to Pace and Argona's (1991) PAR account of the Xerox corporation as a case example of PAR in your own organization.

Action learning

Action learning, associated with the work of Reg Revans (1998), essentially focuses on a learning approach to solving problems at work and in organizations (McGill and Beaty, 1995; Marquardt, 1999; Weinstein, 1999). Through work in peer learning groups, called 'learning sets', participants select issues, examine them, make plans, take action and reflect on that action. In its simplest terms, it is action research without the focus on research and generating usable knowledge or theory.

Action science

Action science is associated with the work of Chris Argyris (Argyris, 1982; Argyris et al., 1985). Argyris places an emphasis on the cognitive processes of individuals' 'theories-in-use', which he describes in terms of Model I (strategies of control, self-protection, defensiveness and covering up embarrassment) and Model II (strategies eliciting valid information, free choice and commitment). Attention to how individuals' theories-in-use create organizational defensiveness is an important approach to organizational learning (Argyris, 1990, 1999; Argyris and Schon, 1996; Senge, 1990; Senge et al., 1994).

Developmental action inquiry

Developmental action inquiry is associated with the work of William Torbert (1987, 1991, 1999; Fisher and Torbert, 1995).

Torbert (1991: 220) defines action inquiry as 'a kind of scientific inquiry that is conducted in everyday life . . . that deals primarily with "primary" data encountered "on-line" in the midst of perception and action'. While Torbert draws extensively on Argyris, he develops the inquiry process by linking the ability to engage in the rigour of action inquiry with stages of ego development. In his view, it is in the latter stages of development that an individual can engage in collaborative inquiry, whereby as the individual reflects on her behaviour-in-action, her behaviour towards others is such that it invites them to do likewise. Such behaviour has implications for the role of leadership and the use of power in creating communities of inquiry (Torbert, 1987, 1989). We will draw on the work of Krim (1988) and Bartunek et al. (1999) as case examples of action inquiry in your own organization.

Co-operative inquiry

Co-operative inquiry is related to action research in that it also focuses on research with people rather than research on people (Heron, 1996; Reason, 1988, 1994a, 1994b, 1999; Reason and Rowan, 1981). In co-operative inquiry, people are co-researchers in that they explore together issues which interest and concern them. Co-operative inquiry is based on the self-determining nature of the human being which means that the co-researchers determine to a significant degree what they do and what they experience as part of the research (Reason, 1994a). This is not to say that everyone has the same practical involvement; some may be initiators, others facilitators, and so on. The participants examine their own experience in collaboration with others who share similar interests and concerns. What is significant is their critical awareness, their quality of reflection and their informed judgements, which contrast with the unexamined projections and consensus collusion of non-critical groups. We will refer to Treleaven (1994) as a case example of co-operative inquiry in your own organization.

Clinical inquiry

In writing about an organization development approach to organizational research, Schein (1987, 1993, 1995) introduces the notion of the 'clinical' approach to research, which is related to action research. For Schein, clinical refers to those trained helpers (such as clinical and counselling psychologists, social workers, organization development consultants) who work professionally with human systems. These trained helpers act as organizational clinicians in that: (a) they emphasize in-depth observation of learning and change processes; (b) they emphasize the effects of interventions; (c) they operate from models of what it is to function as a healthy system and focus on pathologies, puzzles and anomalies which illustrate deviations from healthy functioning; (d) they build theory and empirical knowledge through developing concepts which capture the real dynamics of systems (Schein, 1997). We will draw on Coghlan (1996) as an example of insider clinical inquiry.

Appreciative inquiry

Appreciative inquiry has emerged from the work of Cooperrider, and aims at large system change through an appreciative focus on what already works in a system, rather than a focus on what is deficient (Cooperrider and Srivastva, 1987; Cooperrider et al., 2000; Hammond and Royal, 1998). We will refer to Mellish (1998) as an example of appreciative inquiry in one's own organization.

Learning history

A learning history is a document composed by participants in a change effort, with the help of external consultants who act as 'learning historians' (Kleiner and Roth, 1997, 2000; Roth and Kleiner, 1998, 2000). It presents the experiences and understandings in the words of those who have gone through and/or been affected by the change in order to help the organization move forward. The learning history is an action research process by being an intervention into the organization. This happens when the action research documentation is made available to organizational stakeholders as 'a written narrative of a company's recent set of critical episodes' (Kleiner and Roth, 1997: 173) with the purpose of facilitating learning. Kleiner and Roth (1997) present a framework for how this might be done. The narrative is read by significant stakeholders who contribute to the story from their perspective in a special right-hand column on the page. Those social scientists and 'learning historians' who study the narrative use a left-hand column for their reflection and analysis as the basis for further discussion in the organization. We will refer to Roth and Kleiner (2000) and Kleiner and Roth (2000) as illustrations of learning history.

Reflective practice

Reflective practice refers to how individuals engage in critical reflection on their own action. It is associated with the work of Schon (1983, 1987, 1991; Raelin, 2000). Reflective practice may be a specific dimension of action research, as indeed we will argue in the next chapter, but by and large published accounts of reflective practice focus only on the individual and generally do not consider any organizational dynamics or outcomes related to the individual's action. We will refer to Holley (1997), Lanzara (1991) and Rigano and Edwards (1998) as examples of individual reflective practice.

Evaluative inquiry

Closely related to action research is the process of evaluative inquiry which is a reformulation of traditional evaluation practices through an emphasis on using the process of inquiry to generate organizational learning (Preskill and Torres, 1999). Many of the processes within action research, such as collaborative inquiry, reflection, joint planning and taking action are utilized as interventions to shape how projects are evaluated in order to stimulate organizational learning.

For the neophyte reader these multiple methodologies are confusing. In our view, it is important to emphasize that these different methodologies are not mutually exclusive. They are sets of general principles and devices which can be adapted to different research issues and contexts. Each has its own emphasis and can be appropriately used in conjunction with other methodologies. What is important is that you, as the action researcher, be helped to seek the method appropriate to your inquiry and situation.

CONCLUSIONS

In this chapter we have outlined the foundations of action research as research that is based on a collaborative problem-solving relationship between researcher and client which aims at both solving a problem and generating new knowledge. Irrespective of methodological or epistemological perspective, how to distinguish good research from bad is the key question. Generally speaking, good research is purposeful, its goals are clearly defined and significant, the methodological procedures defensible, evidence is systematically analysed and the 'objectivity' of the researcher clearly evident.

Action research is an approach to research which works at generating data in the field with the concerns of practitioners who want to improve organizations and communities. Regretfully, it has often become a glib term for involving clients in research and has lost its role as a powerful conceptual tool for uncovering truth on which action can be taken. Action research is a form of science, which differs from the model of experimental physics, but is genuinely scientific in its emphasis on careful observation and study of the effects of behaviour on human systems as their members manage change. Action research and the action research cycle will be discussed in detail in Chapter 2.

2

Enacting the Action Research Cycle

In its original Lewinian and simplest form, the action research cycle comprises a pre-step and three core activities: planning, action and fact finding (Lewin, 1973). The pre-step involves naming the general objective. Planning comprises having an overall plan and a decision regarding what the first step to take is. Action involves taking that first step, and fact finding involves evaluating the first step, seeing what was learned and creating the basis for correcting the next step. So there is a continuing 'spiral of steps, each of which is composed of a circle of planning, action and fact-finding about the result of the action' (Lewin, 1973: 206).

These core steps have been articulated differently by different authors, from Stringer's (1999) simple *look, think, act,* to French and Bell's (1999) complex action research organization development framework involving iterative cycles of joint action planning, feedback, further data gathering, diagnosis and action of an external OD consultant with a client system.

THE ACTION RESEARCH CYCLE

For the context of doing action research in your own organization we are presenting an action research cycle comprising a pre-step, context/purpose and four basic steps, diagnosing, planning action, taking action, and evaluating action (Figure 2.1).

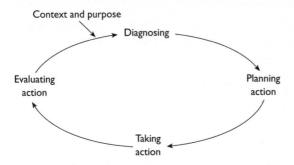

FIGURE 2.1 *The action research cycle*

PRE-STEP: CONTEXT AND PURPOSE

The action research cycle unfolds in real time and begins with an understanding of the context of the project. Why is this project necessary or desirable? In terms of assessing the external context, what are the economic, political and social forces driving change? In terms of internal forces, what are the cultural and structural forces driving change? The assessment of these forces identifies their source, their potency and the nature of the demands they make on the system. Included also is the assessment of the degree of choice as to how the system responds to the forces for change. Once a sense of the need or desirability for the project is identified, then the most useful focus for attention is the definition of a desired future state. The process of defining the desired future state is critical as it sets the boundaries for the purpose of the project and helps provide focus and energy for the later stages.

MAIN STEPS

Diagnosing
Diagnosing involves naming what the issues are, however provisionally, as a working theme, on the basis of which action will be planned and taken. As diagnosis involves the articulation of the theoretical foundations of action, it needs to be done carefully

and thoroughly. While the diagnosis may change in later iterations of the action research cycle, any changes in diagnosis need
to be recorded and articulated clearly, showing how events have
led to alternative diagnosis and showing the evidence and rationale for the new diagnosis on which further action is based. It is
important that the diagnosing step be a collaborative venture,
that is, you as the action researcher engage relevant others in the
process of diagnosis and not be the expert who does the diagnosis apart from others. In Chapter 6 we will focus on how a
project may be framed and in Chapter 8 outline some guidelines
for using diagnostic frameworks.

Planning action

Planning action follows from the analysis of the context and purpose of the project, the framing of the issue and the diagnosis,
and is consistent with them. It may be that this action planning
focuses on a first step or a series of first steps. In Chapter 7 we
will describe how you implement the action research project.
Again we emphasize the importance of collaboration in planning action.

Taking action

Then the plans are implemented and interventions are made.

Evaluating action

The outcomes of the action, both intended and unintended, are
examined with a view to seeing:

- if the original diagnosis was correct;
- if the action taken was correct;
- if the action was taken in an appropriate manner;
- what feeds into the next cycle of diagnosis, planning and
  action.

So the cycle continues (Figure 2.2).

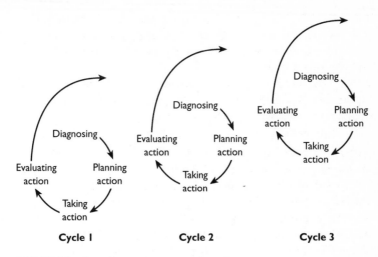

FIGURE 2.2 *Spiral of action research cycles*

META LEARNING

In any action research project there are two action research cycles operating in parallel. One is the cycle we have just described of diagnosing, planning, taking action and evaluating in relation to the project. The second is a reflection cycle which is an action research cycle about the action research cycle. In other words, at the same time as you are engaging in the project action research cycles, you need to be diagnosing, planning, taking action and evaluating how the action research project itself is going and what you are learning. You need to be continually inquiring into each of the four main steps, asking how these steps are being conducted and how they are consistent with each other and, so, shaping how the subsequent steps are conducted. It is the dynamic of this reflection cycle that incorporates the learning process of the action research cycle and enables action research to be more than everyday problem solving. Hence it is learning about learning, in other words, meta learning.

Mezirow (1991) identifies three forms of reflection: content, process and premise. These are useful categories. *Content* reflection is where you think about the issues, what is happening, etc.

Process reflection is where you think about strategies, procedures and how things are being done. *Premise* reflection is where you critique underlying assumptions and perspectives. All three forms of reflection are critical.

When content, process and premise reflections are applied to the action research cycle, they form the meta cycle of inquiry (Figure 2.3). The *content* of what is diagnosed, planned, acted on and evaluated is studied and evaluated. The *process* of how diagnosis is undertaken, how action planning flows from that diagnosis and is conducted, how actions follow and are an implementation of the stated plans and how evaluation is conducted are critical foci for inquiry. There is also *premise* reflection, which is inquiry into the unstated, and often subconscious, underlying assumptions which govern attitudes and behaviour. For instance, the culture of the organization or subculture of the group working on the project have a powerful impact on how issues are viewed and discussed, without members being aware of it (Schein, 1992, 1996a, 1999b).

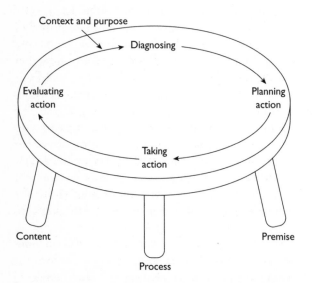

FIGURE 2.3 *Meta cycle of inquiry*

If you are writing a dissertation, the meta cycle is the focus of your dissertation. Remember, the action research project and your dissertation are not identical. They are integrally inter-linked, but they are not the same. The project on which you are working may go ahead irrespective of whether or not you are writing a dissertation. Your dissertation is an inquiry into the project, hence you need to describe both cycles in a way that demonstrates the quality of rigour of your inquiry.

The activities of the meta cycle are not confined to you as the individual action researcher. To add another layer of complexity to the learning cycle, the groups and teams engaged in the action research cycles also attend to the steps of content, process and premise reflection.

The experience of groups and teams in engaging in the action research steps is paramount. As they engage in the activities of diagnosing, planning and taking action they may experience success in some of their activities and not in others. They may experience internal conflict and destructive political behaviour by some members. They may struggle to reach agreement on strate-gies and action and so on. What is important is that groups and teams learn to reflect on their experience in terms of how they function as groups and teams. This involves attending to task issues of how they do the task and relational issues of how they manage communication among themselves, solve problems, make decisions, manage conflict and so on (Schein, 1999a). Interpreting these issues means being able to go beyond personal blame and draw on useful constructs on effective group and team development to take remedial action where necessary and develop effective team processes (Reddy, 1994; Wheelan, 1999). These activities involve content, process and premise as the issues on which they are working are studied, the way in which the teams work is reviewed and underlying assumptions uncovered and examined.

An action research project in an organization is typically not confined to the work of an individual or a team but also involves interdepartmental or inter-team dynamics (Rashford and Coghlan, 1994). Accordingly, we must add yet a further com-plexity to the reflection as content, process and premise reflection are also engaged in by the interdepartmental group. The interdepartmental group experiences the differences between groups, as different groups are separated from one another by what they do, by location and by their interests. Accordingly, any action research work which involves separate departments working together must take account of how each department has its own concerns, its own view of the world, its own political interests in the work of the project and even its own terminology and language. We would argue that interdepartmental group work is essentially intercultural (Schein, 1992).

To add further complexity, the project may involve inter-organizational work, typically called inter-organizational networking. Inter-organizational networking is where member organizations deliberately develop voluntary networks to help deal with complex issues and devise collaborative ways of planning and taking action. As Chisholm (1998) describes, action research is essential for engaging in network development and contributes to planning, action and learning processes. The learning steps of the action research cycle need to be inclusive of

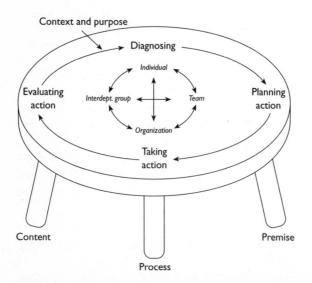

FIGURE 2.4 *Organizational dynamics of action research*

reflection on how different mindsets and political interests are experiencing working together, how they process and interpret that experience and take action accordingly.

Action research involves work with individuals, teams, across the interdepartmental group, organization and between organizations. It also involves work between these levels as an individual has an effect on the team and vice versa, teams affect other teams and an organization's effectiveness is partly dependent on how individuals, teams and the interdepartmental group are in alignment (Rashford and Coghlan, 1994; Figure 2.4). We develop this theme in Chapter 8.

RIGOUR IN ACTION RESEARCH

Rigour in action research refers to how data are generated, gathered, explored and evaluated, how events are questioned and interpreted through multiple action research cycles. In other words, as the action researcher, you need to show:

1 How you engaged in the steps of multiple and repetitious action research cycles (how diagnosing, planning, taking action and evaluating were done), and how these were recorded to reflect that they are a true representation of what was studied.

2 How you challenged and tested your own assumptions and interpretations of what was happening continuously through the project, by means of content, process and premise reflection, so that your familiarity with and closeness to the issues are exposed to critique.

3 How you accessed different views of what was happening which probably produced both confirming and contradictory interpretations.

4 How your interpretations and diagnoses are grounded in scholarly theory, rigorously applied, and how project outcomes are challenged, supported or disconfirmed in terms of the theories underpinning those interpretations and diagnoses.

The value in action research is not whether the change process was successful or not, but rather that the exploration of the data, i.e. how a particular change was managed, provides useful and interesting theory which may contribute to learning on the subject of change management.

What does a good action research project look like? Eden and Huxham (1996) provide an extensive list of the fifteen characteristics of good action research. The foundational characteristics reflect the intentionality of the researcher to change an organization, that the project has some implications beyond those involved directly in it and that the project has an explicit aim to elaborate or develop theory as well as be useful to the organization. Theory must inform the design and development of the actions. Eden and Huxham place great emphasis on the enactment of the action research cycles, in which systematic method and orderliness are required in reflecting on the outcomes of each cycle and the design of the subsequent cycles.

In our view a good action research project contains three main elements: a good story; rigorous reflection on that story; and an extrapolation of usable knowledge or theory from the reflection on the story. These can be put in terms of three questions:

- What happened?
- How do you make sense of what happened?
- So what?

What happened?

As action research is about real time change, its core is the story of what takes place. The action research cycle of the general objective pre-step, and the three main steps of planning, action and fact finding describe how the project is conceived, what is intended, the cycles of action and the outcomes, both intended and unintended. The story must be presented in a factual and neutral manner, that is to say, as if it had been recorded on camera, and so that all the actors could agree on what had taken place. In short, the story is based on directly observable behaviour. Therefore, you need to be able to present evidence to support your narrative. Recorded data in journals and organizational documentation are important supporting evidence.

Accordingly, it is critical that fact be clearly distinguished from value, that the basic story does not contain the author's inferences or interpretations, or at least not without such inferences or interpretations being explicitly identified as such. For instance, if an action research story contains an assertion that a certain group was out to wreck the project, the narrative would need to be clear that there was evidence that the group was trying to wreck the project, rather than it being an inference of the researcher or any party who saw itself as a victim of that group's action. We will explore the role of making inferences in Chapter 3.

How do you make sense of what happened?

The critical process with respect to articulating your sense-making is making your tacit knowledge explicit. This involves not only providing an analysis of what you think is going on in the story, but also of how you are making sense of it as the story unfolds. In other words, sense-making is not only a retrospective process, but is also a process which is concurrent with the story, and, in terms of the action research cycle, actually shapes the story. Hence the image we used in Chapter 1 of the action researcher as actor director. As you report assumptions which you held as the story progressed, you need to show how you tested them, especially if these assumptions were privately held. In terms of our example above, the researcher needs to test whether or not the group which he thinks is out to wreck the project actually intends that.

So what?

The third issue in action research is how the action research project is contributing theory or usable knowledge. As action research is context bound in a particular setting and set of events it needs to have some interest and relevance to the uninvolved reader, the third person readership. Hence the question 'So what?' is pertinent and challenging.

CONCLUSIONS

In summary, enacting the action research cycle involves not only the pre-step of articulating the context and purpose of the project, and the main steps of diagnosing, planning action, taking action and evaluating, but also reflecting on content, process and premise issues in how the action research cycles are undertaken. Both the action research and meta learning are undertaken by individuals, teams, between teams in the interdepartmental groups and between organizations. The rigour of your inquiry is demonstrated by how you expose these activities to critique and how your conclusions are supported by your development of theory or usable knowledge. We will now turn to how you as the action researcher can engage in learning in action.

3

Learning in Action

In this chapter we explore how you, as the insider action researcher, engage in the action research cycles of diagnosing, planning action, taking action and evaluating action. How do you learn in action? How do you attend to what you might be learning as you engage in the issues of your action research project? As answers to these questions, we outline some processes of how adults learn in action and how reflection and journalling may be used to help you realize what you are learning.

Personal learning is available, of course, to anyone who engages in any form of research. For instance, within an ethnographic approach, Young (1991: 393) related how his experience of 'anthropology at home' led him to experience a 'deconstruction of identity', where there emerged a split between the 'anthropological experience of reflexive analysis and the disciplined, controlling requirements of life in the ranks'. Our focus is not on learning *on* action but on learning *in* action.

Lanzara (1991) reflected on the design and adoption of a computer music system in a music faculty of which he was a team member. In the roles of agent of the process and process reflector he experienced himself as both an insider and outsider at the same time. As he helped faculty members carry out evaluations of the project and on their practice, he noted how shifts took place in the story as different understandings of events by different actors evolved. Putting fragments of the story together challenged him to reflect on his own practice, as he found himself feeling vulnerable, not knowing how to deal with the uncertainty generated by the change. He used his reports as a testing device where his story generated responses and reflections from others and helped provoke deeper levels of inquiry.

Learning in action is grounded in the inquiry–reflection process. Inquiry can be focused outward (e.g. what is going on in the organization, in the team, etc.) or inward (e.g. what is going on in me). In Chapter 8 we will outline some conceptual frameworks that provide a basis for organizational diagnosis which are utilized for that outward-focused inquiry and reflection. Here we focus on the introspective activities of inward inquiry and reflection.

The action research project on which you are working is not identical with your own research project. The project on which you are working may, for example, be going on irrespective of whether or not you are studying it. Therefore, it is important to distinguish the action research cycles of the project and the individual experiential learning cycles in which you engage as you participate in the action research cycles.

EXPERIENTIAL LEARNING

As the insider action researcher, you are an actor in the setting of the organization. In contrast with traditional research approaches, you are not neutral but an active intervenor making and helping things happen. Accordingly, a critical feature of action research is how you learn about yourself in action as you engage in first, second and third person inquiry.

How do adults learn (Figure 3.1)? We are presenting four activities: experiencing, reflecting, interpreting and taking action (Coghlan, 1997).

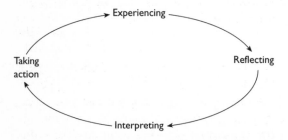

FIGURE 3.1   *The experiential learning cycle*

Experiencing

As the action researcher you experience a great deal as the project goes through its cycles. Some of your experiences are planned, others unplanned. Some are what is done to you by others. Some experiences are cognitive; they occur through the intellectual processes of thinking and understanding. Some occur in feelings and emotions; at times you may feel excited, angry, frustrated, sad, lonely, and so on. Other experiences may be experienced in the body – excited energy, embarrassed blushing, tightness in the stomach, headaches, ulcers or sickness. These three domains – cognitive, feelings and body awareness – are where experiencing occurs and you can learn by attending to them. In your project you are experiencing what it is like to engage in diagnosing, planning action, taking action and evaluating action.

Reflecting

Attending to experience is the first step to learning. The second step is to stand back from these experiences and inquire into them. What is it that has me feeling angry? What is it that I do not yet understand? You are reflecting on your experiences of diagnosing, planning action, taking action and evaluating action in the project.

Interpreting

Interpreting is where you find answers to the questions posed in the reflection. You draw on theories and constructs to help you make sense of your experience. How do you understand what is happening in the processes of diagnosing, planning action, taking action and evaluating action?

Taking action

What do you do as a result of your reflecting and interpreting? It may be that you decide to behave differently the next time you are in a similar situation in order not to repeat the previous experience or in order to create a different outcome. What actions are you taking as a consequence of your reflection on diagnosing, planning action, taking action and evaluating action?

These four activities operate as a cycle where experiencing, reflecting, interpreting and taking action set up another cycle of experiencing and so on. Learning becomes a continuous cycle through life. Learning is not any one of these four activities on its own but each of them together. You need to develop skills at each activity: be able to experience directly, be able to stand back and ask questions; be able to conceptualize answers to your questions, and be able to take risks and experiment in similar or new situations.

You may block learning at each activity. You may view experiencing as something predictable, routine and uninvolving from which you are detached. You may see reflecting as a luxury, an activity for which you do not have any time. You may disregard the conceptualization which accompanies interpreting as something for academics and apart from the 'real world'. You may not engage in taking new action because of a fear of taking risks or of rocking the boat. These are ways in which you may close yourself to learning.

Because the action research project and your own research project are not identical, you are engaging in an experiential learning cycle on the action research cycle (Figure 3.2). So you are experiencing what it is like to engage in diagnosing, planning action, taking action and evaluating, and continuously reflecting and interpreting and taking action within those activities.

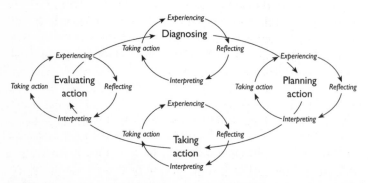

FIGURE 3.2 *The experiential learning cycle in action research projects*

REFLECTION

Reflection is the process of stepping back from experience to process what the experience means, with a view to planning further action (Daudelin, 1996; Kolb, 1984; Raelin, 2000; Rigano and Edwards, 1998). It is the critical link between the concrete experience, the interpretation and taking new action. As Raelin (2000) discusses, it is the key to learning as it enables you to develop an ability to uncover and make explicit to yourself what you have planned, discovered and achieved in practice. He also argues that reflection must be brought into the open so that it goes beyond your privately held, taken for granted assumptions and helps you to see how your knowledge is constructed. In action research, reflection is the activity which integrates action and research. As we discussed in Chapter 2, reflection on content, process and premise is critical to both the action research cycle and to meta learning.

Rigano and Edwards (1998) provided a case example of Vincent, an R&D engineer in a refinery, who worked on improving his own performance through reflection on practice. He used a journal to record his thoughts and reflections, questioned his performance, identified specific skills he could implement and gained some insights into his own learning.

Two critical elements of self-reflection are the ability to critique your own thought processes and to attend to your feelings. With regard to thought reflecting, two useful constructs may be applied to reflecting on how you might be reading behaviour inaccurately. Argyris's ladder of inference plots how meanings and assumptions are attributed to selected observable data and experiences, and conclusions and beliefs are adopted on which actions are based (Argyris, 1990; Friedman and Lipshitz, 1992; Ross, 1994). For example, at a team meeting you make a proposal for action. One of your colleagues, Joe, doesn't say anything. You think he looks as if he is sulking and conclude that he is sulking because his proposal is not being accepted. Accordingly, you decide that Joe is not on your side and that you cannot rely on him for support and subsequently you do not inform him of meetings as the project progresses. What has happened here is that you observed an event, colleagues responding to your proposal. You selected part of that event (Joe not speaking) and added your own interpretations and meaning, which you did not share or test. Then your own subsequent action of excluding Joe from further meetings was based on the beliefs and assumptions deduced from your private meaning. In terms of the image of a ladder, you have ascended the steps of inference, from the bottom rung of what is directly observable behaviour to upper rungs of acting on privately held, untested inferences. The ladder of inference provides a construct for researchers to notice their own privately held inferences and check them.

> *The ladder of inference is explicitly utilized in the creation of a learning history (Roth and Kleiner, 2000). The use of left- and right-hand columns provides a structure for revealing participants' reasoning processes. The learning historians show how they are interpreting events in the right-hand column, which stimulates participants' own reflections in the left-hand column. The presentation of the two perspectives encourages the readers to do their own reflection from both and to become aware of their own reasoning processes.*

The second construct is the notion of cognitive distortions, whereby you may become aware of how you might be prone to distorting reality, particularly when under pressure (Coghlan and Rashford, 1990). You may distort reality when you engage in such activities as: over-generalization, all-or-nothing thinking, mental filtering, jumping to conclusions, emotional reasoning, fortune telling and other similar ways of misperceiving what is happening. Distortions such as these impair your ability to engage in inquiry in action. Emotions as well as thoughts are part of the reflective process. You need to be able to recognize and acknowledge the role feelings play in the formation of judgement and in taking action.

DEVELOPING REFLECTIVE SKILLS THROUGH JOURNALLING

Journal keeping is a significant mechanism for developing reflective skills. You note your observations and experiences in a journal and over time learn to differentiate between different experiences and ways of dealing with them. Journal keeping helps you to reflect on experiences, see how you think about them and anticipate future experiences before you undertake them (Raelin, 2000). It enables you to integrate information and experiences which, when understood, help you understand your reasoning processes and consequent behaviour and so anticipate experiences before embarking on them. Keeping a journal regularly imposes a discipline and captures your experience of key events close to when they happen and before the passage of time changes your perception of them. McNiff et al. (1996) describe some of the useful functions a journal or research diary can have:

- a systematic and regularly kept record of events, dates and people;
- an interpretative, self-evaluative account of the researcher's personal experiences, thoughts and feelings, with a view to trying to understand her own actions;
- a useful way of dumping painful experiences;
- a reflective account where the researcher can tease out interpretations;
- an analytic tool where data can be examined and analysed.

In this book we are drawing on Krim (1988) as an account of action inquiry in his own organization. Krim provided a dramatic account of an action inquiry project in action. He outlined the context of change in a city hall power culture, and described both the political and conflictual dynamics within that culture and the processes of his own personal learning. He described how he noted his reflections and observations on tape while driving home. He described his reflection process in terms of a pyramid of five steps: recording and observing on a daily and hourly basis; a weekly selection and analysis of critical incidents; an exploration of these issues with his academic supervisor; rehearsal and role playing with his supervisor in anticipation of further critical incidents, and a public testing in the real life situation. He reported how this cycle of continuous rehearsal and performance allowed him to improve his performance in highly political and conflictual situations. From this process he received feedback on his management style, particularly how he tended to 'de-authorize' himself, and so he adopted some practical rules of thumb to help him develop new behaviours.

Journals may be set to a particular structure. Kolb's (1984) experiential learning cycle is a useful structure whereby experience, reflection, conceptualization and experimentation form useful headings (Coghlan, 1993a; McMullan and Cahoon, 1979). This format works well. You may learn to attend to details of a situation and with practice can isolate critical incidents which have affected your reactions to events and your judgement as to what to say or do. You develop skills of awareness and introspection. You are challenged in your use of theory and learn to use it in a practical manner. You begin to experience learning as a continuous life task as you apply your learning to future situations.

Another useful framework for journal keeping is Schein's (1999a) ORJI model. ORJI (observation, reaction, judgement, intervention) focuses on what goes on inside your head and how it affects your covert behaviour. You observe (O), react emotionally to what you have observed (R), analyse, process and make judgements based on the observations and feelings (J) and you intervene in order to make something happen (I). Schein pays particular attention to the movement from observation to judgement because he believes that frequently the individual does not pay attention to the reaction stage. In his view, the individual typically denies feelings, short-circuits them and moves straight to judgement and action. You may react to an event by saying to yourself 'That's stupid' – a judgement. What you have probably done is to miss an emotional reaction of feeling threatened by the event. You may not have recognized or acknowledged that feeling of being threatened, yet it is present and governs your judgement. By identifying and attending to feelings (a) as initial reactions and (b) as influencing judgements, you may learn to deal with them and choose whether or not to act on them. Denial of feelings frequently means acting on them without adverting to the fact that you are acting on them. Acknowledgement of feelings to yourself and the subsequent judgement as to the origins and validity of those feelings are critical to learning and change. A journal may be structured around the four ORJI activities.

Schein's ORJI model adds a sophistication to the experiential learning cycle in two ways (Coghlan, 1993a). First, it focuses on a neglected area, namely the spontaneous reaction (which is typically bypassed) to an incident. It provides a framework whereby you may learn to recognize feelings and distinguish them from cognitive processes. Second, it inserts a structured reflection process which works back from action to judgement to reaction to observation. When your view of a situation is not confirmed by how events develop, you may question the original judgement. When you find that the judgement is based on an emotional reaction, then you may question the source of that reaction. With practice you may learn to become more aware of emotional reactions so as to be able to recognize them as they arise, rather than in retrospect. We provide two examples of journalling formats at the end of the chapter.

ACTION RESEARCH SKILLS

Second person research involves core skills at engaging with others in the inquiry process. In his articulation of the dynamics of helping, Schein (1999a) describes several types of inquiry. His first category is what he calls *pure inquiry*. This is where the helper/consultant prompts the elicitation of the story of what is taking place and listens carefully and neutrally. She asks, 'What is going on?' 'Tell me what happened.' The second type of inquiry is what Schein calls *exploratory diagnostic inquiry,* in which the helper/consultant begins to manage the process of how the content is analysed by the other by exploring: (a) emotional processes; (b) reasoning; (c) actions. So the helper/consultant may ask: 'How do you feel about this?' 'Why do you think this happened?' 'What did you do?' 'What are you going to do?' and so on. The third type of inquiry is what Schein calls *confrontive inquiry*. This is where the helper/consultant, by sharing her own ideas, challenges the other to think from a new perspective. These ideas may refer to (a) process and (b) content. Examples of confrontive questions would be: 'Have you thought about doing this?' 'Have you considered that . . . might be a solution?'

Schein's typology of helper/consultant inquiry provides a useful framework for the action researcher. As the action research works at second person research, being skilled at a collaborative approach to problem solving and change management is paramount. The typology is also useful for those who supervise action research (Box 3.1).

SUPERVISING ACTION RESEARCH

Action research is not an impersonal, external and solely intellectual exercise for the researcher. It is, rather, a complex range of personal and social processes, which consequently makes particular demands on those entrusted with the role of acting as supervisors (Marshall and Reason, 1993).

As action research involves the three domains of (a) the individual researcher, (b) collaborative and political involvement with others, and (c) the generation of usable knowledge, supervisors need to attend to all three domains (Reason and Marshall, 1987). With respect to the individual researcher, the supervisor attends to the whole person – how that person's cognitive frameworks and emotional state are shaping action and how they are coping with the demands of the research work in conjunction with their personal lives. With respect to collaborative and political involvement with others, supervisors facilitate reflection and feedback on how that researcher is engaging with others, and provide opportunities for role play rehearsal in anticipation of difficult situations where needed. With respect to generating usable knowledge, this is familiar ground for supervisors and the role with which they are probably most familiar. The adjustment supervisors need to make with respect to action research is that theory generation is primarily extrapolated from insider single case situations, rather than from universal propositions.

Supervisors of action research, therefore, adopt a process orientation, rather than solely providing expert advice on content and methodology. Primary attention is given to *how* the researcher engages in the process of action research. For the supervisor, the supervisory role in action research is akin to process consultation (Schein, 1999a).

Schein (1999a) provides a typology of inquiry interventions which is useful for academic supervisors of action research. He presents three general forms of inquiry:

1 *Pure inquiry*: this is inquiry into the story. Supervisors may pose these sorts of questions: 'What is happening in the situation?' 'Describe it.' 'Tell me more.'
2 *Exploratory-diagnostic inquiry*: this is inquiry into how the researcher is experiencing and understanding what is taking place in the research. Supervisors may pose questions which explore: (a) the researchers' emotional responses – 'How do you feel about that?'; (b) their reasoning process – 'What do you think about that?'; (c) their actions – 'Why do you do that?'
3 *Confrontive inquiry*: this is inquiry that is being shaped by supervisors sharing their own responses and ideas which confront the researchers to consider alternative frames and actions. Such inquiry may focus on *process* – 'Could you . . . ?' and on *content* – 'Have you considered . . . ?'

BOX 3.1 **Supervising action research**

Because as insider researcher you are part of the situation, you may not always act as an external consultant might, that is, be solely the enabler of emergent information and action. Of necessity you have a view of things as they are and what needs to change, and will be expected to share and argue that view. Accordingly, a critical skill for you as the insider action researcher is to be able to combine advocacy with inquiry, that is to present your inferences, attributions, opinions and viewpoints as open to testing and critique (Argyris, 1990; Ross and Roberts, 1994). This involves illustrating inferences with relatively directly observable data and making reasoning explicit and publicly testable in the service of learning. Torbert (1991; Fisher and Torbert, 1995) suggests four 'parts of speech' as useful to the action inquiry role:

- *framing*: explicitly stating the purpose of speaking for the present occasion – what dilemma you are trying to resolve, sharing assumptions about the situation;
- *advocating*: explicitly stating the goal to be achieved, asserting an option, perception, feeling or proposal for action;
- *illustrating*: telling a bit of the concrete story that makes the advocacy concrete and orients the others more clearly;
- *inquiring*: questioning others to understand their perspectives and views.

Putnam (1991) asks if there are recipes which might be useful in helping others to explore their reasoning processes. He suggests that questions like 'What prevents you from . . . ?' and 'What have I said or done that leads you to believe that . . . ?' facilitate a focus on directly observable behaviour rather than on attribution, inference or privately held diagnosis. These interventions may occur in one-to-one or group situations.

CONCLUSIONS

In this chapter we have placed the focus on you as the action researcher. When you engage in the action research cycles of diagnosing, planning action, taking action and evaluating action with others and try to understand and shape what is going on, you are engaging in your own learning cycle activities of experiencing, reflecting, interpreting and taking action (Figure 3.3).

The underlying assumption is that you as the researcher are yourself an instrument in the generation of data. When you inquire into what is going on, when you show people your train of thought and put forward hypotheses to be tested, you are generating data. Accordingly, some of your core skills are in the

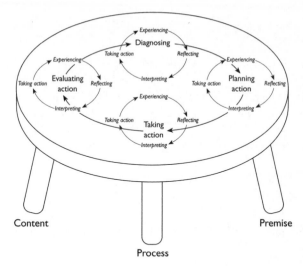

Content

Premise

Process

FIGURE 3.3　*Complex dynamics of action research*

areas of self-awareness and sensitivity to what you observe, supported by the conceptual analytic frameworks on which you base your observations and interpretations. In this respect, your knowledge base in the field of organization behaviour on which you bound your clinical observations is central. In programmes which work from an action research approach, it is likely to be critical that explicit training and education be provided to enable action researchers to develop key interpersonal inquiry and helping skills.

EXERCISE 3.1: KEEPING A JOURNAL

EXERCISE A
Based on Kolb's (1984) experiential learning cycle (Coghlan, 1993a; McMullan and Cahoon, 1979).

1　*Concrete experience.* Describe a concrete event which has taken place in the work situation – what happened, who said/did what, what you felt/said/did, what happened next, what the consequences were. Stick to a single event bounded by time. Be clinically neutral in the description – like a news bulletin.

2   *Reflection.* Now looking back with hindsight – what are your feelings/reactions/observations/judgements on this event? Perhaps now you notice that this has happened before/often. Maybe you are disappointed/angry/pleased with your own reactions at the time. How do you view your reactions/ behaviour? What were the triggers that provoked your reaction?

3   *Conceptualization.* Relate relevant concepts to the experience described and formulate tentative conclusions/ generalizations/hypotheses.

4   *Experimentation.* Suggest action implications for applying/ testing/extending what you have reflected on, with a view to setting some behavioural goals for similar future situations. These are not general resolutions, but specific and concrete actions coming directly from your experience, reflection and conceptualization.

EXERCISE B
Based on Schein's ORJI (Schein, 1999a; Coghlan, 1993a).

1   Take a situation/event where your own behaviour resulted in an unpredicted outcome.

2   Reconstruct the observation you made prior to your intervention, the emotional reaction you had, the judgement you made.

3   Identify which of the emotional reaction, the judgement or intervention may have contributed to the unpredicted outcome.

Other useful approaches to journal keeping are found in Fisher and Torbert (1995), McNiff et al. (1996), Raelin (2000).

4

Researching Your Own Organization

Doing action research in your own organization is a complex process and has its distinctive elements. In this chapter we outline four different forms which insider research can take, depending on the system's and your own commitment to learning in action. Within these frames, how you gain access, manage role ambiguity and use your preunderstanding of the organization are critical.

Researching your own organization involves undertaking research in and on your own organization while a 'complete member' (Adler and Adler, 1987). In membership role methodology, your whole self is engaged in the research process, rather than a defined part. You will be changed through the process. As you are familiar with your organizational setting, you have to create the space and character for your research role to emerge. You need to learn how to look at the familiar through a fresh perspective, develop relationships with people you did not associate with previously, change the nature of pre-existing relationships with them, and become involved with the setting more broadly than hitherto in your functional role (Adler and Adler, 1987; Holian, 1999).

The 'complete member role' as outlined by Adler and Adler (1987) is closest to researchers studying their own organization. Such researchers have an opportunity to acquire 'understanding in use', rather than 'reconstructed understanding'. Riemer (1977) argues that rather than neglecting 'at hand' knowledge or expertise, researchers should turn familiar situations, timely events and/ or special expertise into objects of study. This orientation was partly abandoned by ethnographers during the 'classical era', when participant observation replaced the life history and the emphasis shifted toward greater objectivity and detachment. Participation and, for some, the research process involved becoming a temporary member of the organization in order to observe at first hand how life was lived, was accepted and accorded legitimacy, but subjectivity, involvement and commitment were thrust aside.

The ethnographic role, whether participant-observer or complete membership, and the action researcher role are closely interconnected and sharply distinguished (Schein, 1987). The ethnographic observer attempts to be an unobtrusive observer of the inner life of an organization, while the action researcher works at enabling obtrusive change. Above all, action research is about planned change. This intended change typically involves re-education, a term that refers to changing patterns of thinking and action that are currently well established in individuals and groups. Effective re-education depends on participation by clients in diagnosis, fact finding and free choice to engage in new kinds of action. What is central to this book is how permanent members may undertake action research in and on their own organizations, with permanence being defined in terms of wanting to remain a member within their desired career path when the research is completed.

FOCUS OF THE RESEARCHER AND SYSTEM

In Chapter 3 we distinguished between the action research cycle and the researcher's experiential learning cycle. That distinction was central to naming the core activities of learning in action. In this chapter, we are using the distinction to differentiate between the change project on which the system is engaged and your personal action research project which is to inquire into the change project. As we pointed out, action research in your own organization is opportunistic, that is, you may be selecting an issue for research which is occurring anyway, irrespective of whether or not your inquiry takes place. Hence, we need to distinguish between the two projects, as respective responsibilities may differ. For instance, we know of a case of insider action research in which the researcher is, in effect, doing action research on a major project for which she is responsible. In this case, her supervisor has challenged her to differentiate between the actions of the project and the quality of her inquiry into how that project progresses and what knowledge can be extrapolated. Her research is evaluated on the quality and rigour of her inquiry, rather than on the extent and success of the organizational project which she manages and is accountable to her superiors. In contrast, we know of another case in which the insider researcher is working as an internal facilitator in a change project, but is not responsible for its overall management, a role assigned to a senior project manager.

Accordingly, we need to differentiate between the researcher and the system in and on which the action research is taking place, whether that system be a large organization or a department or unit. In considering how the action research cycle and the experiential learning cycle interlink, we can reflect on the intended goals of both the researcher and the system. As we reflect on cases we know of insider research projects, we notice that the focus of the researcher and system can vary. For instance, we know of an individual manager whose masters action research project was about the organizational change he was leading. His third-party intervention work to manage the politics, power dynamics and conflicts between key protagonists was central to both his managerial role in leading change in his organization and his action research dissertation. His reflection in action was central to his dissertation. At the same time, the members of his organization had little consciousness of the fact that he was doing a dissertation for a postgraduate degree; in their eyes he was simply doing his job. We know of another case of an individual, in the same masters programme, who studied how his organization managed information. In this case, the individual's research focused on what was happening around him and was of great interest to his superiors and other members of the organization, but it did not involve him in any form of conscious self-reflection in action.

Given that there can be a range of foci on the part of both the researcher and system, can these foci be captured in a useful way? In an approach not dissimilar to Torbert (1981), who presented this issue in terms of a grid which juxtaposed no self-study and self-study in action in relation to researcher and system, we understand that research can be viewed along a continuum which reflects the intended focus of the research for both researcher and system (Figure 4.1). We are distinguishing a commitment to intended self-study in action by either or both researcher and system from no such commitment.

FIGURE 4.1 *Focus of researcher and system*

Quadrant 1 is defined by the absence of intended self-study in action by both researcher and system. This is a situation where the researcher is focusing on an issue or problem within the system as if external to herself, and is not engaging in any deliberate self-reflection in action as part of the research process. At the same time, the system itself is not committed to engaging in any intended self-study in action. The researcher may be researching patterns of statistical information, customer preferences, or writing a case history around a particular strategic initiative or a period of time. For the researcher, this is data which is gathered and analysed using established methodologies. This quadrant contains most traditional research approaches, such as qualitative and quantitative studies, ethnography or case writing, as instanced by Young (1991). Since this approach is not the subject of this book, we are not including any further exploration of this quadrant.

Quadrant 2 applies where there is no intended self-study in action on the part of the researcher, while what is being studied is the system in action. We see this as 'pragmatic' action research, which comprises internal consulting projects and action learning. Bartunek et al. (1993) present three case examples of such research. Three of the authors, acting in their organizational managerial capacity, carried out action research projects in their own organizations – in a bank, a manufacturing company and a public utility respectively. The research projects were oriented towards improving operational action, and there is no reported self-study in action on the part of the authors. Frohman (1997) and Friedman (in press) present situations where individuals, typically middle to lower order rank, take initiatives to make changes in their organizations.

Action research in quadrant 2 is typically the type of research, undertaken in MBA programmes, where the focus is manager-led operational projects within a limited, specified time frame. These may well be projects already underway in an organization, and accordingly are opportunistically adopted by manager-MBA students as their action research project. Clearly, such opportunistic adoption is not confined to MBA situations, but may be undertaken by teachers, nurses, social workers, clinicians and like situations where course participants choose pre-existing projects for their own research topic. In these situations, action researchers attempt to bring the action research cycles of inquiry to a project which has not been set up as an action research project. This may make severe demands on action researchers' ability to manage organizational politics. Depending on the origin and scope of the project within this quadrant, the internal researcher may be working with an external consultant hired to facilitate the change.

From their three case experiences of manager-led action research projects, Bartunek et al. (1993) generalize a number of relevant issues and themes:

1 The initial assignment to carry out work that leads to the action research project is likely to come from the manager's superiors and be part of the manager's job description.
2 The other participants in the intervention are likely to be subordinates who need to buy in to the change project.
3 The intervention is likely to be aimed at increased productivity.
4 Managers may find it helpful to constitute a consulting team to assist in the intervention.
5 Data gathering can take place through a variety of formal and informal means.
6 Feedback sessions can be integrated into the work day or conducted separately.
7 The manager is likely to have a personal stake in the outcome of the intervention.
8 The managers were all receiving training in action research while carrying out their interventions.

Quadrant 3 applies where the researcher is engaged in an intended self-study of herself in action, but the system is not. The researcher may be engaging in a study to improve professional practice. She is engaging simultaneously in a process of self-reflection and examining her own assumptions in action and learning about herself as events unfold. The researcher becomes a 'reflective practitioner' (Schon, 1983). As the research agenda is self-selected by the researcher, it may focus on the researcher's job or role within the organization. It may be that the organization does not know of the researcher's personal research agenda. We will draw on cases such as Evans (1997), Holley (1997), Lanzara (1991), Rigano and Edwards (1998) and, more particularly, Krim (1988) who reported how, as initiator and co-ordinator of a new labour–management co-operation programme based on employee participation, he sought to use himself as the key learning strategy, whereby his management style would be central to the inquiry process.

Quadrant 4 is where both the researcher and the system are engaged in intended study in action. The system has made or is making a commitment to change. For example, the system may undertake a system-wide transformational change programme in which everything in the system is open to review, as instanced in the movement to quality of working life (QWL), as instanced by Moch and Bartunek (1990), business process re-engineering and organization development projects or any of those through a learning history approach. In this instance, there is a broad commitment to reflecting on experience and learning. The researcher's role involves being part of this collective reflection and learning, and articulating what is happening. There is active participation by both the system and the individual. In a large-scale system change project, it is likely that there are external consultants, hence the need for insider–outsider collaboration (Bartunek and Louis, 1996). Aspirations to form communities of inquiry in organizations would be located in this quadrant. In this book we will draw on the learning history (Kleiner and Roth, 2000; Roth and Kleiner, 2000) as an example of quadrant 4 action research.

Kleiner and Roth (2000) provided a learning history account of an oil company in which the new CEO set the company on a deliberate course of learning and transformation. The change agenda was initiated through an economic model and then moved to issues of governance, structures, relationships, communication and basic attitudes and behaviour. Fundamental identity and ways of thinking, feeling and acting changed over time. The learning history provides both the observations and reflections on what happened by the participants and the 'analytic' comments by the external learning historians. In the learning history, participants at all hierarchical levels show their perceptions and experiences of what took place. The juxtaposition of multiple views with the view of the learning historians provides a challenging opportunity for the readers and those to whom the learning history is disseminated, particularly the members of the company, to reflect on how the case challenges them to think about their own reasoning processes.

In terms of the focus of this book, we are addressing research projects which are contained in quadrants 2, 3 and 4. The research process itself may provoke a move from one quadrant to another. An action researcher operating in quadrant 2, for instance, may find that the technical problem being researched is a symptom of underlying cultural assumptions, and so its resolution carries more far-reaching implications than was envisaged at the outset. The dimensions of research in quadrant 3 may evolve into quadrant 4. It may be that the researcher's personal development through the research process involves a gradual movement from quadrants 2 to 3. Participants in the masters programme in Management Practice at the Irish Management Institute, University of Dublin, which is a part-time action research oriented programme, reported that they perceived the two-year programme as a journey from quadrants 2 to 3, with quadrant 4 the desired outcome in the long term.

The grid acts as a mechanism for subject selection. You may select a subject based on: (a) a desired outcome for yourself and/or your system, (b) the opportunity for access to areas of the organization; (c) your sense of possession of the level of skill required to work in any particular quadrant. You may ask yourself: What quadrant am I in? What quadrant do I think I am in? Which quadrant am I best at? Quadrant 4 is clearly the most difficult and demanding in terms of conceptual, analytic and practical knowledge and skill.

ROLE, ACCESS AND PREUNDERSTANDING

In our view, the dynamics of doing action research in your own organization, whether in quadrants 2, 3 or 4, involve critical issues of role, secondary access and preunderstanding.

Role duality: organizational and researcher roles

Your organizational role or roles will influence the degree of role confusion or ambiguity that you will experience as an insider action researcher and your ability to cope with your situation. If your sole job in the organization is that of internal change consultant, then you are already a researcher in your own organization. We see this as a single role with low potential for role confusion. Quadrants 2 and 4 of Figure 4.1 incorporate such internal researchers. On the other hand, if your job is that of manager then you are taking on a researcher's role in addition to your managerial job. Hence you have to manage dual roles, manager and researcher, and there is high potential for role confusion. Quadrant 3 of Figure 4.1 is a good example of this situation. Single role researchers, where their job involves research type activities, are quite distinct from dual role researchers where their research activity is a separate role from their standard functional role. In terms of the cases we discuss throughout the book, we can see that Krim and Holian are all examples of dual role researchers whereas Coghlan is an example of a single role researcher.

Pace and Argona (1991) provided an account of an eight-year participatory action research programme in Xerox in which management and trade unions worked together to implement a quality of working life programme. As internal consultants, the authors found themselves in multiple roles: human resource strategists, applied researchers, process champions and interfacers with corporate office, all of which roles had to be integrated and consequently were transparent to management and unions as partners of the project.

Augmenting your normal membership role with the research enterprise can be difficult and awkward, and can become confusing and overwhelming. As a result, in trying to sustain a full organizational membership role and the research perspective simultaneously, you are likely to encounter role conflict (Holian, 1999). Your organizational role may demand total involvement and active commitment, while the research role may require a more detached, more theoretic, objective and neutral observer position. This conflict may lead you to experience role detachment, where you begin to feel an outsider in both roles (Adler and Adler, 1987).

Feelings of detachment can be oriented towards one or other of these roles and increase or decrease as the research progresses. When you are caught between the loyalty tugs, behavioural claims and identification dilemmas you initially align yourself with your organizational role. Elizur (1999) uses the term 'self-differentiation' to review how he, as an insider consultant, managed (a) to contain emotions and to relate to emotionally charged issues in a balanced way; (b) to maintain his own autonomy and self-identity in these situations. Your involvement in the two roles affects your relations with organizational members (Adler and Adler, 1987). The new dimension of your relationship to members and/or your new outside interests set you apart from ordinary members. Your organizational relationships are typically lodged and enmeshed in a network of membership affiliations, as you have been and continue to be a participant in the organization. These friendships and research ties can vary in character from openness to restrictiveness. You are likely to find that your associations with various individuals or groups in the setting will influence your relations with others whom you encounter, affecting the character of the data you can gather from them.

Homa (1998) reflected on what it was like to combine the roles of CEO and researcher. He provided a number of useful pieces of potential advice.

1   *You need to be reasonably on top of your job as it is hard to switch psychologically from management responsibility to research without it. Therefore, selecting the right time in your career to do research is an important choice. You need to possess effective personal organization – time management and the ability to create a distance between work and study – so that you can leave the organization for periods of uninterrupted study.*
2   *You need excellent secretarial support, particularly if you don't do your own typing.*
3   *Over time you need to balance the achievement of being a manager and working through others with the solitary work of a researcher.*
4   *You need a strong management team and a strong and supportive chairman.*

Nielsen and Repstad (1993) cite a number of specific role duality-related advantages and disadvantages of insider research. You may have a strong desire to influence and want to change the organization. You may feel empathy for your colleagues and so be motivated to keep up the endeavour. These are beneficial in that they may sustain your energy and be a drawback in that they may lead to erroneous conclusions. You have to deal with the dilemma of writing a report on what you have found, and dealing with the aftermath with superiors and colleagues, if you do, on the one hand, and doctoring your report to keep your job, on the other. When you are observing colleagues at work and recording your observations, you may be perceived as spying or breaking peer norms. Probably the most crucial dilemma for you as an action researcher in your own organization, particularly when you want to remain and progress in the organization, is managing organizational politics. We will return to this subject in Chapter 5.

Holian (1999) reported how her additional research role added a complex dimension to her organizational role. She found that when organizational members provided information to her 'in confidence' there was some doubt as to whether it was in confidence to her as a researcher or as a senior executive. Merely asking informants as to which hat they saw her wearing at the time did not resolve the uncertainty. If information was provided to her as a senior executive, she may have been authorized or even obliged to act on it to prevent harm to others. If it were provided to her as a researcher, she might not have the right to do so. Whatever the role, organizational members knew she was the same person and knew what they had told her and that she could not forget it.

Secondary access

Primary access refers to the ability to get into the organization and be allowed to undertake research. So as you are already a member of the organization, you have primary access; you are already in. While you have primary access, you may or may not have secondary access, that is, you may or may not have access to specific parts of the organization which are relevant to your research. This is especially true of research in quadrant 3 where the system is not committed to self-study in action. By parts of the organization we mean not only functional areas such as departments, but also hierarchical areas whereby there is restricted access to specific privileged information, which may not be available otherwise. Insider researchers do find, however, that membership of the organization means that some avenues are closed to them because of their position in the organization. Clearly, any researcher's status in the organization has an impact on access. Access at one level may automatically lead to limits or access at other levels. The higher the status of the researcher, the more access she has or the more networks she can access, particularly downward through the hierarchy. Of course, being in a high hierarchical position may exclude access to many informal and grapevine networks. Fundamentally, secondary access means access to documentation, data, people and meetings. In relation to research in quadrants 2 and 4, the system takes responsibility for secondary access because it is committed to self-study.

Krim (1988) worked at developing a successful labour–management participation programme in a US city hall. This was part of his job as Director of Personnel for Human Resource Development. At the same time, he was enrolled in a doctoral programme in a local university and undertook an action inquiry approach to the setting up of the labour–management participation programme as it was happening. Because his research project was part of his job, he had primary access to the actors and events which were shaping the development of the participation programme.

Coghlan (1996) undertook research on change in the region of the Roman Catholic religious order of which he was a member. He was engaging in a longitudinal study of organizational change interventions over an eighteen-year period as doctoral research. As a member he had general primary access to the events of the eighteen-year period under study. As a former member of the central administration team he had more specific access to restricted archives and files. As organization development consultant he had access to the project of reviewing the change programmes in the organization, whereby the granting of permission to access archives and files for research purposes was perceived as an extension of his OD role. At one point he sought and was granted access to more restricted archives, where he considered he needed to scan the minutes of confidential personnel meetings to find further clarification of issues found in less restricted archives.

An important aspect of negotiating the research project is to assess the degree of secondary access to which one is allowed. Dual role researchers may experience more problems than single role researchers. Of course, what is espoused at the outset and then actually allowed may be different once the project is underway and at a critical stage. There may be a significant gap between the aspiration towards 'purity' of research and the reality. How access is realized may depend on the type of research being undertaken and the way information is disseminated.

Negotiating access with your superiors is a tricky business, particularly if the research project aims at good work and not something bland. It raises questions about the different needs which must be satisfied through the project. As an insider action researcher you have needs around doing a solid piece of research which will contribute to your own career and development (first person research, for me). You also have needs around doing a piece of research in the organization which will be of benefit to the organization (second person research, for us) and contribute to general theory for the broader academic community (third person research, for them). Balancing these three audiences is difficult. In general, researchers' superiors have needs around confidentiality, sensitivity to others and organizational politics.

For you, the researcher, who is undertaking research as part of a degree programme or who seeks to publish, a particular issue relating to access is the fact that what is researched will be going outside the organization. Theses and dissertations are read by people external to the organization and are filed in libraries, with their abstracts disseminated to a wider audience. Bartunek and Louis (1996) see this as an 'outsider' role which the insider also plays. In its extreme, organizations can be paranoid about information going outside the organization, or at least be nervous about it.

Young (1991) described the culture of secrecy in the police force and the accompanying suspicion of sociological research. In this culture, as reported by Young, any breach of the secrecy norms was considered a betrayal, the authors seen as traitors and their career prospects put in jeopardy. Hence, Young describes his work as 'writing espionage'.

> *Krim (1988) reported how, when his notes were pilfered from his computer and sent anonymously to a key protagonist, he had to deal with the perception that his academic supervisor was controlling the process from outside the organization.*

In summary, secondary access pertains to the specific nature of the research project. In quadrants 2 and 4 the system takes responsibility for secondary access, and it may be more readily available if all the relevant parts of the system are committed to the project. It is more problematic in quadrant 3, where the system does not necessarily have a commitment to your action research.

Preunderstanding

'Preunderstanding refers to such things as people's knowledge, insights and experience before they engage in a research programme' (Gummesson, 2000: 57). The knowledge, insights and experience of the insider-researcher apply not only to theoretical understanding of organizational dynamics but also to the lived experience of your own organization. Personal experience and knowledge of your own system and job is a distinctive preunderstanding for the insider-researcher, though as Nielsen and Repstad (1993) point out, having a worm's view may be a disadvantage.

One advantage you have as an insider-researcher over an outsider-researcher is that you have valuable knowledge about the cultures and informal structures of your organization. Organizations lead two lives. The formal or public life is presented in terms of its formal documentation – mission statement, goals, assets, resources, annual reports, organizational chart, and so on. The informal or private life is experiential, that is, it is the life as experienced by its members – its cultures, norms, traditions, power blocs, and so on. In their informal lives, organizations are centres of love, hate, envy, jealousy, goodwill and ill will, politics, infighting, cliques and political factions, a stark contrast to the formal rational image which organizations tend to portray. You have valuable experience of this, though you don't know it all. While this knowledge is an advantage, it is also a disadvantage, as you are likely to be part of the organization's culture and find it difficult to stand back from it in order to assess and critique it. You may need to be in tune with your own feelings as an organizational member – where your feelings of goodwill are directed, where your frustrations are and so on.

Nielsen and Repstad (1993) outline some examples of such experience and preunderstanding. You have knowledge of their organization's everyday life. You know the everyday jargon. You know the legitimate and taboo phenomena of what can be talked about and what cannot. You know what occupies colleagues' minds. You know how the informal organization works and whom to turn to for information and gossip. You know the critical events and what they mean within the organization. You are able to see beyond objectives which are merely window dressing. When you are inquiring you can use the internal jargon and draw on your own experience in asking questions and interviewing, and be able to follow up on replies and so obtain richer data. You are able to participate in discussions or merely observe what is going on without others being necessarily aware of your presence. You can participate freely, without drawing attention to yourself and creating suspicion.

There are also some disadvantages to being close to the data. When you are interviewing you may assume too much and so not probe as deeply as if you were outsiders or ignorant of the situation. You may think you know the answer and not expose your current thinking to alternative reframing. You may find it difficult to obtain relevant data because, as a member, you have to cross departmental, functional or hierarchical lines or because, as an insider, you may be denied deeper access, which might not be denied an outsider.

Coghlan's (1996) preunderstanding was based on three elements. First, there was his membership of the organization and basic familiarity with its members, ideology, values, culture, ministries and language or terminology. Second, there was his experience as a member of the region's central administrative team in which he worked as an internal organization development consultant in projects of strategy and change.

Through this element, he was personally familiar with many of the interventions, and the reports and files pertaining to those interventions. Third, his education, training and experience in organization development provided a familiarity with the constructs for reflecting on and conceptualizing change processes.

Political knowledge was a critical element of preunderstanding in Krim's (1988) city hall organization. However, as he points out, his understanding of the informal knowledge-based power structure was inadequate when he underestimated the connection power of one particular individual whom he tried to replace. That person was able to muster considerable support to resist Krim's efforts to replace her and severe confrontational conflict ensued.

Schein (1992, 1999b) describes organizational culture as patterns of basic assumptions which have been passed on through generations of organizational members and which are unnoticed and taken for granted. Accordingly, the approach to uncovering cultural assumptions is a dialogue between organizational members and an external process consultant who facilitates the exploration of what assumptions underlie artefacts and values. As an insider-researcher you may need an external consultant to help you make sense of your experience. The academic supervisor may play this role. Krim (1988) reported how, in his meetings with his academic supervisor, he would role play critical incidents. These role plays were important in his reflective learning process.

A practical issue you have to deal with is that you may be too close to the issues and the people in the organization and so you have to work more consciously and explicitly at the process of inquiry. If you have been trained in a particular discipline or are familiar with a particular function you may not be open to seeing problems from other perspectives. You may be too close to the people and the situations you are researching. What if the research involves critiquing your friends or close colleagues? It may be difficult for you to stand back from the situation and question your own assumptions, which heretofore have been unquestioned.

Coghlan (1996) interviewed the executive leaders who had formed and led particular parts of the change processes. When he was interviewing the executive with whom he had personally worked closely, he noticed that he contributed to the conversation more than he had done in the interviews with the other executives. He realized that because he was so close to this particular situation he was tending to shape the outcome and so needed to build in a balancing mechanism. Accordingly, he sent a draft of the chapter dealing with the particular period under review to that executive and interviewed him a second time. In this way his account and analysis of the events of the period was amended through further dialogue with this protagonist.

Role duality and secondary access tend to be research project specific and organizationally dependent, whereas preunderstanding tends to be researcher-specific. Therefore, preunderstanding is not directly linked to the quadrant schema. Preunderstanding, as the word suggests, is what the insider brings to the research process.

ACTION RESEARCH AT HOME

Not all action research in your own organization is done at places of work. The following example illustrates action research at home.

Goode and Bartunek (1990) described a self-initiated action research project in an apartment complex, where Goode initiated a process to address a problem of direct personal concern. In the apartment complex where Goode was a resident, there were problems relating to mail delivery and security. Single efforts to address resident concerns had been unsuccessful. Goode approached several concerned residents, discussed the problem with them and explained action research in order to foster an environment which enabled collaboration and the search for multiple causes of the problem, rather than the unitary blaming of the complex's caretakers, which was common. Goode then formulated a plan for gathering information which involved: (1) producing an informational letter which she distributed to all residents; (2) conducting preliminary meetings with some of the residents and the caretakers; (3) conducting an informational session with anyone interested in participating; (4) interviewing all interested individuals. All these actions took place and the data generated was analysed under such headings as: organization strengths, existing mail security problems and existing group-level structures and problems. A feedback session was held at which task forces were formed to address particular issues and actions implemented.

Goode and Bartunek reflect on this case in terms of two issues. First, this case is an example of action research in an under-bounded system. As this subject is not central to the theme of this book we will not reflect further on this point. Second, and the point which concerns us in the context of action research in your own organization, is how the action researcher initiated research in an organization where she had a personal stake. Goode and Bartunek point to two roles the action researcher played. One role was that of a long-term participant in the system, which meant she shared the concerns of the fellow residents and had credibility. The other role was a short-term consultant role where her knowledge of action research provided guidance for the process. She was willing to take an educative, directive and participative approach to enable the resolution of problems and the emergence of new structures.

CONCLUSIONS

In this chapter we have reflected on the subject of doing research in and on your own organization. Researching your own organization involves undertaking research in and on your own organization while a complete permanent member, which in this context means both having insider preunderstanding and access, and wanting to remain a member within your desired career path when the research is completed. In undertaking action research in and on your own organization, the commitment to learning in action by both the system and yourself is a useful defining construct. If the research project is accompanied by the system's commitment to learning in action, then secondary access is easier. If your organizational role is that of internal consultant, then your research role is integral to that role. If on the other hand you are a manager, then you are taking on the researcher role in addition, which may create confusion.

As an insider action researcher you are engaged in first person research, using your preunderstanding of organizational knowledge and organizational studies for your own personal and professional development. You are engaging in second person research by working on practical issues of concern to your organization in collaboration with colleagues and relevant others. You are engaging in third person research by generating understanding and theory which are extrapolated from the experience.

Doing action research in your own organization involves: (a) clarifying the action research project in terms of both your own and the system's commitment to learning in action; (b) managing issues of role and secondary access.

PART II

IMPLEMENTATION

5

Managing Organizational Politics

While doing any research in an organization is very political (Punch, 1994), doing research in and on your own organization is particularly so. In this chapter, we examine the politics and ethics involved in doing action research in your own organization.

THE POLITICS OF RESEARCHING YOUR OWN ORGANIZATION

Clearly any form of research in any organization has its political dynamics. Political forces can undermine research endeavours and block planned change. Gaining access, using data, disseminating and publishing reports are intensely political acts. Take for example, the act of diagnosis, which we discussed in Chapter 2 and will revisit in Chapter 8. Diagnosis is never a neutral act; it rarely affects stakeholders in the same way. Some may benefit and some may be harmed because it exposes weaknesses in performance. So while action research diagnosis is a collaborative activity, raising certain questions and applying judgements to particular issues may have severe political implications.

Therefore, doing action research in your own organization is political. Indeed it might be considered subversive. Weinstein (1999) lays out the subversive characteristics of action research in your own organization. It examines everything. It stresses listening. It emphasizes questioning. It fosters courage. It incites action. It abets reflection and it endorses democratic participation. Any or all of these characteristics may be threatening to existing organizational norms. Cooklin (1999) refers to the insider change agent as the 'irreverent inmate' who is a supporter of the people in the organization, a saboteur of the organization's rituals and a questioner of some of its beliefs. While as the action researcher you may see yourself attempting to generate valid and useful information in order to facilitate free and informed choice so that there will be commitment to those choices in accordance with the theory and practice of action research (Argyris and Schon, 1996), you may find that, as Kakabadse (1984) argues, what constitutes valid information is intensely political.

Accordingly, you need to be politically astute in deciding to engage in action research, becoming what Buchanan and Badham (1999) call a 'political entrepreneur'. In their view, this role implies a behaviour repertoire of political strategies and tactics and a reflective self-critical perspective on how those political behaviours may be deployed. Buchanan and Boddy (1992) describe the management of the political role in terms of two activities, performing and backstaging. *Performing* involves you in the public performance role of being active in the change process, building participation for change, pursuing the change agenda rationally and logically, while backstage activity involves the recruitment and maintenance of support and the reduction of resistance. *Backstaging* comprises skills at intervening in the political and cultural systems, through justifying, influencing and negotiating, defeating opposition and so on. Because you are an insider you have a preunderstanding of the organization's power structures and politics, and are able to work in ways which are in keeping with the political conditions without compromising the project or your own career.

As you engage in your action research project, you need to be prepared to work the political system, which involves balancing the organization's formal justification of what it wants in the project with your tacit personal justification for political activity. Throughout the project you will have to maintain your credibility as an effective driver of change and astute political player. The key to this is assessing the power and interests of relevant stakeholders in relation to aspects of the project. One particular manager may have a great deal of influence with regard to budget allocation, but little influence with regard to strategic decision making.

Managing political relationships

In order to be able to manage the content and control agendas of the action research project and the power-political processes of influencing and ensuring the legitimacy of your project, you need to be able to manage your superiors, peers and colleagues (Kotter, 1985). Building on the work of Greiner and Schein (1988), we have identified ten key power relationships (Figure 5.1). All of the ten key power relationships need to be considered and managed when carrying out a quadrant-3-type action research project where the system is not committed to self-study in action. The first two relationships may not be of great importance for quadrant 2 and 4 research projects where the system is committed to self-study in action.

First, there is your relationship with your sponsor. It is most likely, if you have a middle or low organizational rank, that you have a sponsor who provides permission and primary access to undertake the research, both in the initial and latter stages of the

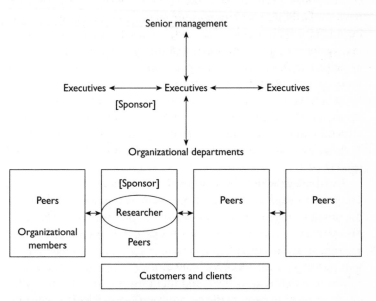

FIGURE 5.1   *Power relations for the action researcher*
(Adapted from Greiner and Schein, 1988.
Reprinted with permission of Prentice Hall Inc., Upper Saddle River, NJ)

project. Where the research is part of a degree programme, the sponsor grants you permission to have time off to attend the course, take study leave and use organizational materials for research. The sponsor may be your immediate superior within the same department. In this case the relationship may be close and supportive. The sponsor may be elsewhere in the organization, in a position of higher management. You need to work at maintaining this relationship as the continuation of the research project may depend on it (Weidner, 1999). This may become particularly difficult if it emerges that the sponsor is a source of problems within the organization. You need to keep your sponsor abreast of developments and seek his or her counsel. That way you keep him or her informed and on your side.

Second, there is the sponsor's relationship to other executives. Your credibility and access may depend on the sponsor's status and standing within the organization. If the sponsor is not considered favourably by other executives, it may have a negative effect on how your research project is perceived. The sponsor's power relationship with other powers in the organization is critical in gaining acceptance for that research from higher levels of management or administration. Secondary access may be granted or denied at this level. You may have to leave the sponsor to do your access negotiation for you or you may be allowed to approach these other executives yourself. This will depend on the nature of the project. It may be that you are helpless in this regard. Whatever the project, you will have to work independently at establishing the credentials and value of the research project.

Third, there is the relationship of executives with each other. The power dynamics between departments or individual heads of departments may be a relevant feature in promoting or blocking the research. If you are from one department, that may inhibit co-operation from other departments. This may be the most significant political force for you as insider researcher, and the one over which it may be most difficult to exercise control. The key is to build personal relationships with significant persons in other departments so that they will co-operate. Perhaps some of them will be members of your project team.

The fourth relationship exists between you and significant others. Whatever the relationship between the sponsor and other executives, you must be able to establish your own relationship with significant others, many of whom may be key executives. This is particularly relevant if you wish to interview senior executives and ask what might be experienced as awkward questions. If your sponsor falls from favour, you will need to have established relationships with significant others in order to maintain your profile and project.

Friedman (in press) described the case of Marc, a middle manager, who addressed the behaviour of his CEO at a meeting of managers. At a time of closures and employees being fired, and consequent low morale and uncertainty in the organization, Marc questioned the CEO's strategy of promotions in the light of firings and low morale. The CEO subsequently sent for him privately and rebuked him strongly for questioning him in public.

The fifth relationship is between executives and others in higher management. Senior management at a corporate level may undermine the research or withdraw consent. The relationship tends to be remote, in that the executives are not likely to know you personally. It is usually unnecessary for them to have any detailed knowledge of your project. You may not have access to these people, so you may find it difficult to exercise influence over them.

The sixth relationship is between executives and organizational members. This relationship includes relationships between management and workers and management and trade unions so that the research is accepted by the relevant parts of the organization. The research project may fall victim to ongoing organizational relationships, where employees use a lack of co-operation with you as a power tool to express dissatisfaction with some unrelated aspect of organizational life with which there is a dispute in order to gain political leverage. In these situations you are powerless and dependent on others for the resolution of the dispute.

Seventh, there are the interdepartmental relations, where some departments have more power than others, where there are different subcultures, all of which may work for or against a research project. If, for example, you work in the head office or corporate centre, you may have to deal with the attitudes of those in regional offices who prejudiciously view anyone from the corporate office. The key is to establish a personal relationship with significant persons who will co-operate with you.

The eighth relationship is that of the researcher with subordinates on whom you may be relying for significant information. Subordinates may feel the need to be less than honest with their boss, who is undertaking the research. It may be that your own behaviour and management style are critical factors in the issues under investigation, and so subordinates may be reticent in providing accurate information or feedback. In such a case, where you are a superior, having a third party gather data may be essential.

Nuttall (1998), in his reflection on his joint roles of Head of Site and researcher, noted the political complexity of requesting subordinates to answer questionnaires which have been distributed by the boss. He concluded that his own participative management style, built up over six years, resulted in a trusting relationship between his subordinates and himself and enabled them to speak freely and provide the information he sought. At the same time, he was aware that he needed to counter the influence of bias, and so he engaged a neutral research assistant to conduct some interviews, and then to compare the transcripts. He further reflected that care in the management of power was a critical skill for the researcher who is also one in authority.

The ninth relationship is with customers or clients who may be the ultimate beneficiaries of the research or who may be involved in the actual research process. Approaching clients and customers has political complexities as it may raise expectations about the service provided to them.

Finally, there is the relationship between you and your peers. Engaging in research which involves your peers, some of whom may be friends, is particularly sensitive and may make the research process stressful. If peers and colleagues are the subject of observation and comment, they need to be informed and actively involved. They need to be protected from possible retaliation by superiors. At the same time, you need to be wary of how you can be biased in favour of peers and colleagues, be seduced by the closeness of the relationship and hence be unable to reflect and critique. Peers, colleagues and superiors may be asking the following sorts of questions: What is she observing? What is she writing about me? Am I being criticized? For those unfamiliar with an action research approach the idea of doing research in the everyday job may be hard to grasp. How can you work and include research at the same time? This question comes not only from a limited notion of what constitutes research but also from a fear of being criticized in writing behind one's back.

Pace and Argona (1991) reported how, in their internal consultancy role of champions of the quality of working life process, which involved collaborating with external consultants and unions, they lost credibility with many middle managers.

The management of the research project involves attention to all ten relationships by building support and involving key others.

Holian (1999) reported how she felt unprepared for the backlash which resulted from surfacing 'undiscussables' within the organization related to cover-ups, perceived abuse of power, nepotism, harassment, allocation of rewards and unfair discrimination. While these issues were deeper, more shocking and troubling than anticipated, she reflected that she was not adequately prepared to look after herself or others when the backlash came. Consequently, she was not able to balance the multiple roles of researcher, senior executive and programme facilitator, and, after one last stand-up fight with some of her fellow senior executives, she resigned.

Ramirez and Bartunek (1989) reflected on role conflict explicitly in their case of an insider action research project in a health-care organization. They cited two specific instances. In one instance, they noted that the insider action researcher had to deal with the twin role of facilitating meetings while at the same time acting as a department head whose status was junior relative to other participants. The second role conflict was more explicitly political. Other organizational members spread rumours about the action researcher to the effect that she was engaging in the research to set up a position for herself. The researcher's experiences of being the recipient of such political behaviours caught her off guard and were hurtful to her.

Friedman (in press) reflects that in cases of individual research where issues are non-technical, there are likely to be insurmountable obstacles and high degrees of defensive routines. How then do you work as a 'political entrepreneur' engaging in the public performance and backstaging activities? Kakabadse (1984) presents six useful guidelines:

1 *Identify the stakeholders.* This means identifying those who have a stake or interest in the project and its outcomes and approaching them so as to identify their intentions.
2 *Work on the comfort zones.* This means working on those behaviours, values and ideas which a person can accept, tolerate or manage. As long as these are not threatened, people will be able to focus on wider concerns.
3 *Network.* This means going beyond formal hierarchies or structures where necessary to coalitions of interests which may exert greater influence on key stakeholders than the hierarchical structure.
4 *Make deals.* The making of deals is common in organizations as individuals and groups agree to support one another on a particular issue in return for support on others. This is a common way of reaching agreement on policies.
5 *Withhold and withdraw.* It may be useful on occasion to withhold information in order not to fuel opposition, though you would not want to withhold information constantly. It is also useful on occasion to withdraw from conflictual situations and let others sort out the issue.
6 *If all else fails.* Kakabadse recommends that you need to have some fall-back strategies if all else fails. These obviously depend on the demands of the situation and what you can personally handle and manage.

Friedman (in press) provides more specific guidelines:

1   Describe your own reality image and situation as concretely as possible.
2   Ask senior and middle management if this explanation accurately fits as they see it.
3   If there are significant differences, inquire into the sources of these differences.
4   Continuously inquire into the reasoning behind actions.
5   Design strategies dealing with the current situation and similar future ones.

Lewin's force field analysis is a most useful tool to use for assessing and constructing interventions with respect to organizational political forces. As it is presented in many organization development texts, force field analysis is a technique created by Kurt Lewin for problem solving or managing change. It is based on the assumptions that in every situation there are forces driving change and forces restraining change, and that an emphasis on reducing restraining forces is more effective than increasing driving forces. While a force field might look like what we might do in listing reasons for and against taking an action, it is actually quite different. Reasons for and against are static and rational; they have to be justified. In force field analysis, forces impinging on a situation are listed. Hence, with regard to organizational politics, a force field of political driving and restraining forces may provide you with a useful insight into what is going on and help you construct interventions to reduce restraining forces. We provide a structure for using it at the end of the chapter.

Researchers often think that they have little power in the research process because they are dependent on powerful others for access. Others may see the researcher as powerful because she is knowledgeable, has initiated the research and is selecting whom to involve. In effect they may see the researcher's view of reality as being given public visibility. Accordingly, therefore, we need to examine some ethical issues of doing action research in your own organization.

ETHICS

Ethics, in the context of research, have typically been discussed in terms of the traditional empirical research paradigms, where the focus is on researchers using subjects to obtain information to meet their own individual research objectives. Within these paradigms, ethics are taken to refer to not doing harm, not breaching confidentiality, not distorting the data, and so on. Action research is built on participation within the system being studied. This participation is based on the assumption that the members of the system understand the process and take the significant action. Hence, ethics involves authentic relationships between the action researcher and the participants in the research – individuals, groups, organizations and communities. Bentz and Shapiro (1998) place an emphasis on 'mindful inquiry', whereby the researcher engages in activities to prepare a space for inquiry to occur and for participants to occupy. The creation of a space is itself inquiry. Hence, the researcher looks at the possible effects of the inquiry on the participants, the self of the researcher and on the potential future of the relationship between the researcher and participants. The researcher's assumptions have an effect on all stages of the research project – topic selection, method of analysis, and so on. As Torbert (1991) puts it, action inquiry involves a certain developmental maturity in researchers to collaborate with others and expose their thought process to public testing.

> *Homa (1998), in his reflection on the CEO as researcher, pointed to important ethical issues at the design stage of the research. As the CEO as researcher may be seen as a 'cerebral detective', it is important to use information to enhance the research and not to cast a shadow over employee career prospects when he encounters information which would change his perception of individuals and departments. He stresses confidentiality for those who contribute to the research, unless permission is given to divulge their views.*
> *The role conflict between her senior executive position and her action researcher role that Holian (1999) experienced when organizational members provided her with information*

which she did not know if she could use in her researcher role, and which she thought she should use in her executive role, created an ethical dilemma for her. As her research subject was ethical decision making she faced a double dilemma; a content one for her organization and a process one for the research. She established and participated in a co-operative inquiry group comprising people of decision-making roles from a diverse range of organizations. The members of this group discussed ethical issues they were experiencing and encouraged one another to reflect on their own experience and find new ways of working with ethical issues in their own organizations.

Here are some ethical issues you will need to consider and resolve:

- Negotiating access with authorities and participants.
- Promising confidentiality of information, identity and data.
- Ensuring participants the right not to participate in the research.
- Keeping relevant others informed.
- Getting permission to use documentation which was produced for other institutional purposes.
- Maintaining your own intellectual property rights.
- Keeping good faith by showing you are someone who can be trusted and always checking with others for any misunderstanding.
- Negotiating with those concerned how you will publish descriptions of their work and points of view.

CONCLUSIONS

If you are engaging in action research in your own organization, politics are powerful forces. You need to consider the impact of the process of inquiry, who the major players are, and how you can engage them in the process. Ethics involve not only not deceiving or doing harm, but being true to the process. This does not mean telling everyone everything or being politically naïve, but rather recognizing who the key political players are and how they can value the research by participating in it. We will return to this subject in Chapter 7, where we explore how these political relationships may be enhanced to implement the research project.

It may seem that political dynamics are the major obstacle to doing action research in your own organization, which may put you off. At the same time there are those who revel in political behaviour and enjoy the cut and thrust of attempting to make a difference through their action research project.

EXERCISE 5.1: FORCE FIELD ANALYSIS

Force field analysis comprises five steps.

Step 1   Describe the change issue and the desired direction of the change.

Step 2   List the political forces driving change and those restraining it in a diagram which has the forces in opposition to one another.

Step 3   Give a weighting to the forces, those that are stronger and more powerful than others.

Step 4   Focus on the restraining forces and assess which of the significant ones *need* to be worked on and those which *can* be worked on.

Step 5   Develop plans for reducing these forces.

6

Framing and Selecting Your Project

In this chapter we discuss how you might frame and select an action research project. When you 'frame' an issue you are naming it, and by naming it you are focusing on how you might set up its analysis and set the criteria for evaluation. Framing is a heuristic process, by which we mean that the definition of an issue already includes elements of the solution. 'Reframing' is the process whereby you question an existing frame and possibly discard it in favour of a different one (Bartunek, 1988). Then, new frames of reference need to be created to reframe the issues in such a way that problem solving can be effective.

FRAMING THE ACTION RESEARCH PROJECT

Framing an issue can be a complex process. As we saw in the bank case in Bartunek et al. (1993), it may be that what is attractive as a research project is a practical operational issue – there is a recurring problem, which management or superiors would like researched and a solution found. In the case of the bank, the project was identified as one of improving relationships between the bank and a client. Such a research project can clearly meet criteria of being useful, particularly to management, and achievable in the research time frame and manageable for the researcher. As the research progresses it may also turn out that this apparent operational problem is more complex than it appears, requiring key people to alter their mandates and ways of thinking. We saw an example of this in the manufacturing case in Bartunek et al., where the development of an integrated manufacturing system involved radical changes in how the company did business.

The complexity of issue identification and selection illustrates that the search for an appropriate issue to study is difficult. How do you get a sense of the array of possible issues which may be addressed? By using the term 'array' we are acknowledging the existence of a wide and diverse set of issues all vying for research attention. That is not to say of course that all issues are immediately apparent to you. Some may be blatantly obvious while others may go unnoticed unless attempts are made to uncover organizational members' perceptions of key issues. Not every issue will volunteer itself automatically for resolution. It is human perception that makes the difference, thus leading us to conclude that organizational actors' interpretations are pivotal in this whole process.

While acknowledging the existence of a wide and diverse array of issues, it is important to understand that any issue once selected for attention may be embedded in a set of related issues (Beckhard and Harris, 1987). You are then confronted with choices concerning boundaries and are obliged to choose between what can be achieved within the time specified for your research and available resources.

Thinking in terms of issues, rather than problems or opportunities, which warrant attention is vital as language and labels are of the utmost importance at the outset (Cooperrider and Srivastva, 1987; Dutton et al., 1983). For example, framing proposed research initiatives in the context of addressing problems or opportunities carries some inherent risks. Framing an issue as a problem may influence who gets involved in problem resolution. It may be that organizational members embrace problems with a sense of loss, wondering about the organization's ability to reach a satisfactory resolution and often preferring to remain somewhat detached and uncommitted. The action research project may be challenging traditional procedures and ways of thinking.

Ramirez and Bartunek (1989) reported that the collaborative approach of the OD project in the health-care organization was a radical departure from standard practice, and that it was the first directed focused attempt in the entire hospital to apply a collaborative model to problem solving involving nursing, medicine and administration.

Treleaven (1994) initiated an inquiry process into the work-ing lives of women at the university in which she was a staff development manager. From a sense of the inadequacy of the formal affirmative action training programmes, she made per-sonal contact with women around the campus and issued an open invitation to form an inquiry group which would focus on leadership. The group comprised academics from most of the faculties and formed what they called 'listening circles' as the members engaged in storytelling from their own experi-ence, with a particular emphasis on their experiences as women in a male-dominated culture. Treleaven describes the method in terms of 'creating a space' where inquiry could take place by setting up a framework and enabling structures where interested participants could engage in collaborative processes. That involved many telephone conversations with potential members of the group as she explored and recruited partici-pants. From the group process, three domains of outcome were identified: (a) individual, personal and professional development; (b) the potential for long-term organizational change where, by drawing attention to the gendered culture of a masculinist organization, new forms of leadership and par-ticipation which are inclusive of women were constructed; and, (c) the research outcomes relating to the substance of the research, the methodology and the participation of the mem-bers as co-researchers.

Using the word 'problem' as distinct from 'opportunity' may also lead to convergent thinking (Dutton et al., 1983). The mental effort expended on problem resolution may restrict the range of alternatives considered, blinding organizational mem-bers to the possible existence of novel solutions. In a similar vein, the use of the word 'opportunity' may lead to divergent thinking as this label has a greater sense of gain associated with it. Organizational members may feel a sense of excitement about tackling a significant opportunity which may have the potential for creativity.

Mellish (1998) reported how a newly appointed planning dean in a university was given the task of developing a new faculty out of four existing departments, which were aligned to two existing faculties. In order to achieve the necessary transformation of strategy, structures and culture, she involved the 160 academic and general staff, who represented the multiple subcultures and strong views about the future of their respective areas and disciplines, in an appreciative inquiry process. Through a series of meetings and workshops, they worked through the phases of appreciative inquiry and produced a plan which was accepted and endorsed by the university, and transitions plans were accepted and implemented. In Mellish's view, the appreciative inquiry approach, rather than a problem-oriented one, enabled the participation and consensus to achieve the desired outcome.

Finally, language and labels are important as they have the potential to influence risk-taking behaviour (Dutton et al., 1983). It may be that thinking in terms of opportunities cultivates a risk-taking culture, while thinking in terms of problems cultivates a risk-averse culture. If you think with an opportunity mindset, then you are less likely to embark on a witch-hunt looking for someone to blame, as there isn't anything for which to blame them, while the mindset associated with problems embraces the notion of finding a scapegoat. It seems obvious from the above that there is merit in thinking in terms of issues without any attempt to subclassify such issues in the first instance.

What becomes important then is to uncover the issues which are viewed by organizational members as key and warranting attention at any point in time. With regard to those issues which involve complex organizational change, many of them may initially fall into the category of operational problem solving. As already noted, not all issues are blatantly obvious and it is therefore important for you as the researcher to get a sense of both the obvious and less obvious. It may be that the obvious is but an outward manifestation of a deeper issue which organizational members are not so willing to embrace publicly. Identification of these deeper issues may point to the need for inquiry into the fundamental assumptions which keep a problem recurring. What if the obvious only seems that way due to being ill-informed on the nature of the issue at hand? Could it be that the obvious has become so as it embraces the language of dissent and reflects the preoccupations of organizational members with consequences without ever reflecting on root causes?

As insider action researcher you need to go with the story as it evolves. As the initial questions and data demonstrate that they are inadequate for addressing the issues, you work at keeping inquiry active. You are continually testing whether consensus exists concerning the array of issues which could be addressed (Dutton and Duncan, 1987; Dutton and Jackson, 1987). Such an array may be constructed having considered organizational members' perceptions of key issues. It may embrace a healthy diversity of thinking among organizational members or, alternatively, it may point to significant pockets of conflict in certain issue domains. Change triggers discussion, debate and arguments between people who champion competing ideas and proposals. Such discussion provides useful data and is desirable in order to expose different ideas to public scrutiny and examination (Buchanan and Badham, 1999).

Regardless of what the array of issues reflects, it is impossible to construct research without leaving one's own familiar world and entering into the world of others through open and honest dialogue. This of necessity means that you are willing to explore key concepts and themes and attempt to construct the perceptions of others concerning the range of issues. It involves understanding why organizational members frame such issues in the first instance, while simultaneously capturing causal relationships (Dutton et al., 1983).

We have seen that Krim's (1988) highly politicized organization did not favour or support such open inquiry. Hence, Krim's action inquiry approach was, in Torbert's (1991) view, most appropriate for insider research as it threw light on the political, organizational and personal barriers for the researcher as he worked in the social role defined within the system. We also saw how Holian's (1999) project on ethical decision making opened up what were perceived as undiscussable issues and led to conflict, resulting in Holian's resignation from the organization.

No issue in an organization is context free (Dutton and Ottensmeyer, 1987). Uncovering issues necessitates establishing not only multiple versions of 'the real facts', but also understanding the role which history and experience have to play in organizational members' perceptions of these facts. In a similar manner, any given issue may be embedded in a system of political behaviour which it is critical to understand if issue resolution is ever to be negotiated. Krim (1988) reported how he was told that open sharing of information in city hall was dangerous and foolhardy.

Holley (1997) sought to inquire into how she could contribute to a living educational theory through an exploration of values in professional practice. As a head of department in a UK second level school, she sought to explore with other teachers, by means of an appraisal system, how to enable them to reflect on their contribution to learning in the school. Independently, the management of the school introduced a classroom monitoring system, where teachers would be observed in action and assessed in terms of a checklist. This outraged Holley as she experienced this monitoring approach as a violation of her educational values. She then worked at attempting to respect, understand and listen to explorations of other teachers as they tried to make sense of their work within the prescribed monitoring system. Her superior told her she was soft and that dialogue was not objective and hard edged. However, she managed to subvert the monitoring system to some degree and work with a colleague in an inquiring, reflective mode.

The process of identifying issues may be characterized as fluid, dynamic and emergent (Dutton et al., 1983). It is fluid in the sense that it is difficult to establish precise boundaries and when such boundaries are established they are often subject to change. It is dynamic in the sense that the core focus is subject to continuous revision as understanding deepens. It is emergent in the sense that issues appear over time. These key characteristics point to a process which is further characterized by the unfolding nature of interpretation and reinterpretation, making extensive use of organizational members' judgements and revision of judgements based on insights gained from new and existing data, stimuli and perceptions.

*Ramirez and Bartunek (1989) described how rumours were
spread around the health-care organization in order to dis-
credit the action researcher to the effect that she was using the
project to set up a position for herself.*

*Krim (1988) was advised by key colleagues that he was not
handling power differences very well. He was given a copy of
a pamphlet, 'How to Swim with Sharks', and advised to be
more 'shark-like'.*

Of immediate importance then, to you, is the need to gather and
organize these data, stimuli and perceptions of yourself and others.
The subsequent sense-making process points to the need for you to
have good organizational and analytical capabilities. Krim (1988)
kept a journal of his reflections and observations and used his academic supervisors to test them in a safe environment.

In the context of deriving meaning, it is useful at this juncture in
the research process to frame issues in broad categories without
attempting to attach a single dominant interpretation to any issue.
The existence of multiple interpretations concerning an issue must
not be eliminated. Capturing multiple and diverse interpretations
adds to a deeper, richer picture of the issue at hand and holds the
key to more effective resolution for the long term. In the power culture of city hall, Krim (1988) was in constant conflict regarding the
interpretation of events. For example, the fact that he made notes
on meetings was perceived as a tactic for manipulation.

There is an inherent danger in the process of attempting to
simplify an issue by reducing ambiguity at an early stage. Such
endeavours are manifested by ignoring some interpretations of an
issue and attempting to attach a single dominant interpretation
with a view to aiding resolution. Such a process may seem quite
rational to the researcher who may be eager to get on with the
task at hand. Rationality plays a role in the analysis stage but one
cannot assume that rational analysis will lead to resolution.
Resolution often involves a process of negotiation, embracing a
sense of give and take where political interests warrant careful
management. Neglecting political influences is a recipe for
inaction as any proposed course of action may be planned to
death and eventually be stillborn.

Attaching a dominant interpretation to an issue is not necessarily bad as long as you remain cognizant of the fact that other interpretations exist and are willing to test such interpretations as the need arises. It is equally important to understand the basis for such dominance. Does the interpretation reflect a shared mind at all or almost all organizational levels, or does it reflect the shared mind of a particular group such as, for example, management or trade unions?

The extent to which a dominant interpretation of an event or issue is shared or otherwise by organizational members is important for you as the researcher, as it implies that different strategies must be employed to aid issue resolution. Where a dominant interpretation is widely shared you are more likely to gain a greater degree of commitment to the resolution process with lower levels of political activity, at least at the early stages. Where the interpretation reflects the mind of a specific group, you need to be cognizant of the fact that other groups may not share that interpretation and may choose never to share it for political reasons. Friedman (in press) presents projects initiated by individuals on a continuum, with technical issues at one extreme and nontechnical at the other. In his view technical operational issues are easier to support, while non-technical issues are harder to influence and are embedded in organizational defensive routines. Krim (1988) reported that the most powerful union leader did not support the labour–management co-operation programme, while other government personnel did.

> *Quinlan (1996), a clinical psychologist in a mental health unit, sought to inquire into his own professional practice as well as how roles played in multidisciplinary teams and the wider organization interacted and shaped professional practice. He sought to collaborate with his colleagues to inquire into 'complex cases', as instanced in the case of an individual client so as to develop mutual collaboration. This co-operative inquiry venture into good practice, which he referred to as 'working with downstairs', had only partial success. After some time, his peer group unilaterally decided to hold meetings with other professionals, rather than continue with the client-focused case meetings that he had initiated. At the same time he was working with senior management, which he calls 'working*

with upstairs'. In this group the focus was on power and inter-action was marked by confrontation. Accordingly, his desire to remain in the organization was both an enabling and restrain-ing force on the way he constructed and dealt with power dynamics.

Finally, it is important when categorizing issues that each is framed in the context of its implicit and explicit assumptions, any known causal relationships and any predictive judgements concerning the speed of issue resolution (Dutton et al., 1983). Making assumptions explicit aids the resolution process as orga-nizational members develop a shared understanding of the issue being addressed in terms of its history, scope and possible out-comes. Establishing causal relationships helps to place an issue in context by grounding it in organizational reality while simul-taneously establishing how organizational members attribute certain outcomes to root causes. Outlining predictive judgements attaches a sense of urgency or otherwise to the issue at hand.

SELECTING THE RESEARCH PROJECT

Having identified a range of issues, you are confronted with selecting an issue or issues for immediate attention in the context of a specific research agenda. Before making a final selection you are well advised to reflect on each issue identified from personal and organizational perspectives with a view to establishing:

- the degree to which it offers an opportunity to experiment with existing and/or newly acquired knowledge;
- the degree to which it offers opportunities for personal growth and learning;
- the degree to which issue resolution offers the possibility of increasing your profile within the organization;
- the balance between personal gain and organizational gain in the event of successful resolution;
- the degree to which the issue may be resolved within known resource and time constraints.

CONCLUSIONS

Framing and selecting an action research project is complex. What appears clear at the outset may lose its apparent clarity as the project unfolds. How you frame and subsequently reframe the project may hold important learning for you. The critical issue for you is to be able to frame and select a project from a position of being close to the issue. The acts of framing and selecting your action research project are themselves action research learning cycles. In other words, you do your initial framing, reflect on how that framing fits or not, articulate some understanding of why that framing fits or does not fit and then take action accordingly and so test that situation. Similarly, you make your initial selection, test it and adapt it according to the data generated by the selection and framing processes.

EXERCISE 6.1: QUESTIONS FOR FRAMING AND SELECTING

As I look at my organization/section in which I work:

1 What questions arise out of my experience to which I would like to search for answers?
2 What might be the answers to these questions?
3 What do I think might be the underlying causes of the situation for which I have these questions?
4 What alternative answers might exist?
5 Where do I fit into the situation as defined by the question?
6 What would other members of the organization think of me working on this issue?
7 What opposition will I encounter?
8 Where are the sensitive issues?
9 Who needs to be involved? Whose support do I enlist?
10 Where would be a good place to begin?
11 How will I engage in uncovering the data?

Implementing Your Action Research Project

In this chapter we will explore how you may implement an action research project. In Chapter 3, we outlined the skills you require. The action research process in your own organization follows the action research cycle introduced in Chapter 2. This involves:

1 Systematically collecting research data about an ongoing system relative to some objective or need.
2 Feeding the data back to relevant others.
3 Conducting a collaborative analysis of the data.
4 Planning and taking collaborative action based on the diagnosis.
5 Jointly evaluating the results of that action, leading to further planning.

So the cycle is repeated.

THE PROCESS OF CHANGE

How do you go about implementing the action research cycle in a planned way in a large system? While actor-directors go with the story in their movie-making, they also create and follow a script. The process whereby the action research agenda is identified and worked through has been well articulated by Richard Beckhard (Beckhard and Harris, 1987; Beckhard and Pritchard, 1992). Beckhard's framework has four phases:

1 Determining the need for change and the degree of choice.
2 Defining the future state, after the change has taken place.

3   Assessing the present in terms of the future to determine the work to be done.
4   Managing the transition state.

As we discussed in Chapter 5, doing action research in your own organization is intensely political and involves you in concurrent and sometimes conflicting roles. We think that it is important to remind you that managing the political system at every step is more important than any rigid adherence to an idealized picture of how these steps might work.

Determining the need for change

The preferred starting place is to inquire into the context for change in the organization, unit or subunit (Pettigrew, 1987). It may seem obvious that naming the need for change and its causes is essential. The forces for change may be coming from the external environment, such as global market demands, developing customer needs, and so on. They may be coming from the internal environment, such as budget over-runs, low morale among staff, excessive dysfunctional political intergroup rivalry, and so on. The diagnosis of these forces identifies their source, their potency and the nature of the demands they are making on the system. These forces for change have to be assessed so that major change forces are distinguished from the minor ones.

A second key element in evaluating the need for change is the degree of choice about whether to change or not. This is often an overlooked question. Choices are not absolute. While there may be no control over the forces demanding change, there is likely to be a great deal of control over how to respond to those forces. In that case there is likely to be a good deal of scope as to what changes, how, and in what time scale the change can take place. The action research cycle enables shared diagnosis into how these forces for change are having an impact and what choices exist to confront them. The outcome of determining the need for change is to ask a further question, which is whether first or second order change is required. By first order change is meant an improvement in what the organization does or how it does it. By second or third order change is meant a system-wide change in the nature of the core assumptions and ways of thinking and acting. The choice of whether to follow a first or second order change process may be as much determined by organizational politics as by the issues under consideration. How the key organizational actors interpret the forces for change and how they form their subsequent judgement as to what choices they have are important political dynamics.

Defining the desired future

Once a sense of the need for change has been established, the most useful focus for attention is to define a desired future state. This process is essentially that of articulating what the organization, unit or subunit would look like after change has taken place. This process is critical as it helps provide focus and energy because it describes the desires for the future in a positive light. On the other hand, an initial focus on the problematic or imperfect present may over-emphasize negative experiences and generate pessimism. Working at building consensus on a desired future is an important way of harnessing the political elements of the system.

Assessing the present in terms of the future to determine the work to be done

When the desired future state is articulated, you then attend to the present reality and ask 'What is it in the present which needs changing in order to move to the desired future state?' Because the present is being assessed in the light of the desired future, it is assessing what needs changing and what does not. It may judge that, for the change effectively to take place, a change in current structures, attitudes, roles, policies or activities may be needed. As any change problem is a cluster of possible changes, it may need to group particular problems under common headings: i.e. HRM policies and practices, service delivery, information management, reward systems, organizational structure, design, and so on. Then it describes the problem more specifically and asks: 'Which of these requires priority attention? If A is changed, will a solution to B fall easily into place? What needs to be done first?' This step is about taking a clear, comprehensive, accurate view of the current state of the organization, involving an organizational diagnosis which names:

- the priorities within the constellation of change problems;
- the relevant subsystems where change is required;
- an assessment of the readiness and capability for the contemplated change.

Another element in describing the present is to describe the relevant parts of the organization that will be involved in the change. This description points to the critical people needed for the change to take place. This is an explicit consideration of the political system and where you draw on your skills as a 'political entrepreneur'. Examples of who needs to be involved might include specific managers, informal leaders, IT specialists, and so on. Their readiness and capability for change must be assessed. *Readiness* points to the motivation and willingness to change, while *capability* refers to whether they are able, psychologically and otherwise, to change.

Managing the transition

This step is what is generally perceived as being the actual change process though, as we have seen, preparation for change is equally essential. The critical task is to move from the present to the future and manage the intervening period of transition. This transition state between the present and the future is typically a difficult time because the past is found to be defective and no longer tenable and the new state has not yet come into being. So, in essence, the transition state is somewhat particular, as the old has gone and the new has not yet been realized, and so needs to be seen and managed as such.

There are two aspects to managing this transition state. One is having a strategic and operational plan which simply defines the goals, activities, structures, projects and experiments that will help achieve the desired state. As no amount of change can take place without commitment, the second aspect is a commitment plan. The commitment plan focuses on who in the organization must be committed to the change if it is to take place. There may be particular individuals whose support is a prerequisite for the change and a critical mass whose commitment is necessary to provide the energy and support for the change to occur. The political dynamics of building commitment involve finding areas of agreement and compromise among conflicting views and negotiating cooperation (Fisher and Ury, 1986; Ury, 1991).

It is at the management of transition stage that you are likely to make most use of a group which works with you as the core project team. While you are the one doing the dissertation, this group is an organizational project group which contains both technical competence and hierarchical status to manage the project. Hence there is a need for you to be able to build and maintain the team (Wheelan, 1999).

Beckhard's four-step process is the quintessential action research process as it involves continuous interaction between diagnosis, planning, action and review in order to move a change through a system (Figure 7.1). Action research has a large degree of messiness and unpredictability about it, in that it is research on real-life action. As the story unfolds unforeseen events are likely to occur. Environmental events may create a crisis in the organization; fellow key actors may change and so on. The action researcher as actor-director is both creating and acting a script.

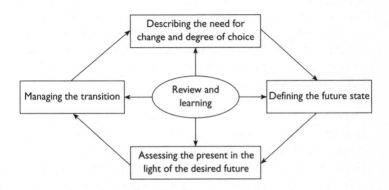

FIGURE 7.1 *The process of change*

REVIEW AND LEARNING

The critical dimension to action research is how review is undertaken and managed. Review is essentially reflection on experience and in any such reflection the critical questions are asked, not to evoke guilt or blame, but to generate learning as to what is taking place and what needs to be adjusted. If review is undertaken in this spirit then the likelihood of individual or team defensiveness can be lessened and learning can take place.

It might appear from these pages that action research is a logical and clinical process, where individuals and groups move through the action research steps in a rational, albeit politically aware, manner. However, such approaches are not exclusive. It is not uncommon for researchers to utilize storytelling, drama or photography as a core process of their data generation (Marshall, 1995).

> *Evans (1997) studied her own practice as a deputy head of a large second level school in the UK. Within a hierarchically organized institution, she worked with teachers collaboratively, enabling the creation of a learning community through dialogue in which they took ownership of their own development, established value position and supported one another. She created case studies out of her experiences in the school and presented them as stories to the group. For example, she composed one story titled 'Just Tell Me What to Do' out of her own experience. The other teachers were able to relate to the story as it reflected school culture. This and other stories enabled the teachers to reframe their perspectives and to explore new perspectives together.*

DATA GENERATION AS INTERVENTION

In action research data comes through engagement with others in the action research cycles. Therefore, it is important to know that acts which are intended to collect data are themselves interventions (Schein, 1995). So asking an individual a question or observing him at work is not simply collecting data but is also *generating* learning data for both you, the researcher, and the individual concerned. In short, you are not neutral. Every action, even the very intention and presence of research, is an intervention and has political implications across the system. Accordingly, it is more appropriate to speak of data *generation* than data gathering.

For you as the insider action researcher, data generation comes through active involvement in the day-to-day organizational processes relating to the action research project. As the researcher in your own organization, you are an inconspicuous observer, as your presence is taken for granted. Your observations are made as a member of the organization in the day-to-day interactions with colleagues and others. Not only are data generated through participation in and observation of teams at work, problems being solved, decisions being made and so on, but also through the interventions which are made to advance the project. Some of these observations and interventions are made in formal settings – meetings and interviews; many are made in informal settings – over coffee, lunch and other recreational settings.

You will need to document your reflections for all these occasions. This is, of course, a sensitive process as appearing to take notes may create suspicion. A useful rule of thumb is to adopt what others are doing. If at a meeting most people take notes, then it is acceptable for you to take notes. If no one is taking notes, then you do not take notes. In that case, you try to jot down your reflections afterwards, as soon as possible, while events are fresh in your memory.

When you observe the dynamics of groups at work – for example, communication patterns, leadership behaviour, use of power, group roles, norms, elements of culture, problem solving and decision making, relations with other groups – you are provided with the basis for inquiry into the underlying assumptions and their effects on the work and life of these groups (Schein, 1999a, 1999b). As you are dealing with directly observable phenomena in the organizations with which you are working, the critical issue for you is how to inquire into what you are observing and, at the same time, be helpful to the system. For example, at a team meeting you may notice all sorts of behaviour which you suspect affects how the team goes about its work – people not listening to each other, wandering off the agenda and so on. If you make an intervention into these areas you are aiming to focus on what is useful for the advancement of the action research project, rather than what you have observed. Without this discipline you may reflect what you have observed, but the observation may not be owned by participants in the system because it does not meet their needs as experienced or appears to be showing how clever you are in observing these things. For you, observation and inquiry into how the systemic relationship between the individual, the team, the interdepartmental group and the organization operates is critical to the complex nature of organizational problem solving and issue resolution (Rashford and Coghlan, 1994).

You may consider using some form of survey instrument. An action research approach suggests that data-gathering tools need to be designed to fit both the organizational setting and the purpose of the research (Cunningham, 1993). While surveying employees by questionnaire as to their views on some aspects of their work or the organization tends to be seen merely as a method of collecting information, it is more important to see how it is an intervention. The reception of a questionnaire by employees may generate questioning, suspicion, anxiety, enthusiasm – all of which are real data for you. If you ignore this you may be missing a key element of how the organizational problem exists and does not get solved and indeed what issues lie ahead in the research process.

In a similar vein, interviewing in action research is not simply a tool for collecting data (Cunningham, 1993; Schein, 1995). As we have pointed out, asking someone a question or a series of questions is a data-generating intervention. Interviewing in action research tends to be open ended and unstructured, focusing on what the interviewee has to say, rather than confirming any hypothesis the action researcher might have. In Chapter 3, we presented a typology of interview techniques, pure inquiry, exploratory-diagnostic inquiry and confrontive inquiry (Schein, 1999a). As we emphasized in that chapter, combining inquiry with advocacy is a critical skill for the insider action researcher.

While a distinction is made between the study of formal documentation (what Gummesson calls 'desk research') and interviews, Gummesson (2000) makes the point that these are artificial distinctions as the researcher is faced with a continuous flow of data. Secondary data are both numeric and textual and developed for some purpose other than helping to solve the action research question in hand. You need to evaluate this data on the basis of its relevance to the research question, its availability and accuracy. In order to have confidence in the worth, validity and reliability of the data, you need to consider the following questions for each archival source:

1   Who collected the data?
2   When was it collected?
3   What was collected?
4   Why was it collected?

Studying relevant documentation can be an important part of organizational research. Access to documentation is integrally linked to the level of access to engage in research. Reports, memos, minutes of meetings and so on may be highly confidential and access to them may depend on the degree to which an organization's management is willing to grant access to the inside researcher. Other documentation may be held in archives in the organization or in libraries. Hill (1993) provides both a general introduction, and practical guide, to using archives.

> One of the central issues for Coghlan (1996) at the outset of his research was to discover what relevant documentation existed and how it could be found. As he had been a member of the organization's central administration team on two occasions he had both a general sense of the chronology and significance of events and a good deal of prior information as to what had happened, when and what documentation was extant. Documentation reviewed fell into three groupings:
>
> 1   Documentation circulated to the organization and accessible to all members, such as letters from the executives, texts of executive addresses given on special occasions, policy statements, and reports of some task forces.

2   *Documentation internal to the central administration: staff memos, minutes of staff meetings, reports of consultations, terms of reference for task forces and consultations, and summaries of policy developments for internal use.*

3   *Confidential documentation.*

An important element of Coghlan's preunderstanding as a former member of the central administration team was his inside knowledge of both the content of the research and the system in the archives. In one instance it was by leafing through an unmarked folder that key material was uncovered accidentally; he knew the material existed but could not find it in catalogued files. There were many instances of undated documents, the dates of which could only be pieced together by inside knowledge of when these issues were under consideration. There were instances where the author knew from his experience that certain files/documents existed, but could not find them in the archives. On many occasions these were found in other parts of the office complex.

Coghlan worked from his experience and prior knowledge of the history of policy development in the organization. In asking what was in the archives, he knew that minutes of meetings, drafts of policy, letters and addresses, many reports and so on existed. He had used them himself in his work as a staff member and internal consultant. The issue of how comprehensive and systematic the documentation would be in facilitating a large-scale research project was unknown. In general the documentation was more than adequate in providing the information required to put data together for the purposes required by his research.

Coghlan's position as a member of the organization and an internal consultant was significant in the data gathering. He had unrestricted access to the archives. He had extensive knowledge of the period and experience of the issues under research and his familiarity with the administration offices facilitated the uncovering and evaluating of relevant material.

What were the criteria by which the documentation was judged to be relevant? As the purpose of studying the documentation was to uncover primary sources, the criteria were that the documents studied showed what intentions were articulated, what was done and what was said about what was done, etc.

HOW DO YOU KNOW WHEN TO STOP?

Action research projects which act as dissertations typically have an inbuilt time schedule. Especially within single-year or two-year masters programmes, you are expected to do your action research project within a designated time period in order to meet the requirements of the programme to which you are attached. Accordingly, you may take your submission deadline, the amount of time you are going to give yourself for writing the dissertation and work back to where your organizational story will end. In many respects, the decision you make as to when your story will end is arbitrary. At the same time it is important to set a date after which, whatever takes place, however exciting and relevant, will not be included in your story.

When completion deadlines have more flexibility, your decision to stop is still arbitrary and may depend on your judgement as to the extent that your project has yielded sufficient learning.

CONCLUSIONS

In this chapter we have explored how you might go about implementing an action research project. We have shown that, after determining the need for it, it is useful to work at articulating a desired future before getting into details of what to do and how to build commitment to the action. Accordingly, you need to keep in mind that everything you do is an intervention and be sensitive to the impact which asking questions and observing have on participants. You need to manage the politics of the situation at all times.

▶

EXERCISE 7.1: THE PROCESS OF IMPLEMENTATION

Step 1 Determining the need for change:
- What are the external forces driving change?
- What are the internal forces driving change?
- How powerful are these forces?
- What choices do we have?

Step 2 If things keep going the way they are without significant intervention:
- What will be the predicted outcome?
- What is our desired outcome?

Step 3 What is it in the present that we need to change in order to get to our desired future – what is done, how work is done, structures, attitudes, culture?

Step 4 What are the main avenues which will get us from here to there?

What are the particular projects within those avenues – long term, medium term, short term?

How do we involve the organization in this project? Where do we begin?

What actions do we take to create maximum effect, medium effect, minimum effect?

How will we manage the transition?

How do we build commitment? Who is/is not ready/capable for change? How will we manage resistance?

Who will let it happen, help it happen, make it happen?

Do we need additional help – consultants, facilitators?

Step 5 What review procedures do we need to establish? How do we articulate and share what we are learning?

8

Making Sense: Using Frameworks to Study Organizations in Action

We now turn our attention to the process of making sense of organizational dynamics by presenting some features of organizational diagnosis and the use of frameworks. Organizational dynamics and the use of frameworks are subjects in themselves (Bolman and Deal, 1997; Burke, 1994b; Harrison and Shirom, 1999). There are innumerable frameworks which can be found in standard textbooks and in the writings of those authors who have created them. For instance, within the field of business strategy you may be familiar with frameworks which enable you to analyse the competitive nature of an industry or relative position of a firm within an industry. Within marketing, you may draw on frameworks which help position a product or service. In every field and subject area there are frameworks which enable you to make sense of the current situation and predict outcomes. In relation to doing action research in your own organization, we highlight the systems approach and give particular attention to constructs of organizational learning and change. We are not attempting to provide a list of such frameworks, but rather aiming at providing an introduction to their use.

ORGANIZATIONAL DIAGNOSIS

We use the term *diagnosis* to refer to investigations that draw on concepts, models, and methods from the behavioural sciences in order to examine an organization's current state and help clients find ways to solve problems or enhance organizational effectiveness. (Harrison and Shirom, 1999: 7)

Underlying the principle of organizational diagnosis is a notion of organizational health which organizational clinicians are using to compare with the present situation (Schein, 1997). Accordingly, frameworks which postulate key organizational variables and relationships are important diagnostic tools.

Organizational frameworks are presentations of organizations which help categorize data, enhance understanding, interpret data and provide a common shorthand language (Burke, 1994b). They typically describe relationships between organizational dynamics, such as purpose, strategy, structure, control systems, information systems, rewards systems and culture, and help organize data into useful categories and point to what areas need attention.

Some guidelines are useful for selecting and using frameworks. Weisbord (1988) advises that frameworks should have four features: that they be simple; fit members' values and highlight things they consider important; validate members' experience by putting recognizable things in a new light; and that they suggest practical steps. Burke (1994b) provides three guidelines for selecting a framework. One is that you should adopt a framework you understand and with which you feel comfortable. The second is that the framework selected should fit the organization as closely as possible, be comprehensive enough to cover as many aspects of the organization as appropriate and be clear enough for members of the organization to grasp. The third is that the framework should be sufficiently comprehensive to enable data gathering and interpretation without omitting key pieces of information. In a word of caution, Burke points out that you may become trapped by your frameworks, so that your way of seeing becomes a way of not seeing. So as an action researcher you need to critique the frameworks you use.

SYSTEMS THINKING AND PRACTICE

A significant contribution to situation analysis is systems thinking and practice. Systems thinking refers to seeing organizations as a whole, made up of interrelated and interdependent parts.

The human body is a good example of a system, whereby bones, muscles, tissues and organs perform interdependent and interrelated functions. While we might dissect the body and make an analysis of any particular part, the body's functioning depends on a holistic view of how all the parts work together. Similarly, organizations may be viewed as systems, in which planning, control, structural, technological and behavioural systems are interdependent and interrelated.

Understanding organizations as open systems, that is being dependent on its external environment for its survival, has been well established in organizational theory for many years (Hanna, 1987; Katz and Kahn, 1978). What has received less emphasis is the 'recursive' systems model that represents organizations as patterns of feedback loops and sequences of interaction which link and integrate elements of a system (Balle, 1994; McCaughan and Palmer, 1994; Senge, 1990). In systems thinking, linear cause and effect analysis is replaced by viewing patterns of interaction which mutually influence each other.

'Dynamic complexity' refers to situations where a system is complex, not because of a lot of detail but because of multiple causes and effects over time (Senge, 1990). In situations of dynamic complexity, systems thinking provides a perspective of viewing and understanding how a system is held together by patterns of action and reaction, relationships, meanings and hidden rules and the role of time. In order to inquire into how a system functions, you can engage in systemic questioning (McCaughan and Palmer, 1994):

- *Establishing circuitry*: When A does . . . what does B do? What does A do next?
- *Establishing patterns*: What patterns are evident over time?
- *Exploring meaning*: What are the meanings held in the system? What are the common meanings attributed to events and actions?
- *Exploring covert rules*: What unarticulated and hidden rules govern behaviour?
- *Exploring the time dimensions*: How time delays have an impact on the system.

It is not easy to find answers to questions posed by systemic questioning. Formulation of tentative working explanations as to what is happening in the system – the circuitry, patterns, covert rules, meanings and time – may uncover the dynamic complexity of the system and involve many iterations of collaborative inquiry before finding explanations which fit.

Systems thinking and action research

Systems thinking and the action research cycle play complementary roles. In a systems approach to action research, tentative explanations are being formed as the story unfolds. These explanations are tentative frames to articulate the elements of the system in order that they may be understood and to consider interventions to change them, where required. A very useful way of formulating systemic explanations is through the use of diagrammatic representation. When cycles of action and their consequences are drawn in a diagram, the patterns of the system may be illuminated. Both the act of attempting to represent the system diagrammatically and the diagram itself are essential elements of the learning process. The very act of drawing the system's diagram is a learning process of explanation formulation and testing (Anderson and Johnson, 1997; Bawden, 1991). In traditional research approaches, intuition is frequently placed against reasoning and considered alien from a research process. In Senge's (1990) view, the systems approach holds the key to integrating intuition and reason, because intuition goes beyond linear thinking to recognize patterns, draw analogies and solve problems creatively.

CHANGE AND LEARNING

As change and learning are central to action research, it is important for the action researcher to draw on knowledge of how change and learning take place (Burke, 1994a; Schein, 1996b, 1999b). How change and learning take place applies not only to individuals, but also to groups, between groups and to organizations (Coghlan, 1997; Rashford and Coghlan, 1994). Change theory has evolved from Lewin's (1966) model that the change process has three stages or sets of issues: being motivated to change, changing, and making the change survive and work. Lewin argues that a system must unlearn before it can relearn and that attention to all three stages is equally critical. Lewin's research and theory of change has been a formative influence on the emergence of the theory and practice of organization development (French and Bell, 1999), and on organizational change as a process of re-education (Coghlan, 1994).

Any action researcher in an organization needs to understand how people in organizations can resist change (Coghlan, 1993b). An important starting place is that resistance is a healthy, self-regulating manifestation which must be respected and taken seriously by the action researcher. Rashford and Coghlan (1994) present two psychological reactions to the initiation of a change. When a change agenda is first presented people may *deny* its relevance. When denial is no longer sustainable it may be replaced by *dodging*, which is an effort at diverting the change. Denial and dodging are natural reactions to a change agenda, especially when it is unexpected. In Rashford and Coghlan's view, they are a prelude to *doing* and *sustaining*, when the change agenda is accepted and implemented.

Coghlan (1996) applied the Lewin-Schein change model to the change process of his organization. He noted that the unfreezing period, in which the issues and reasons for change were raised and promoted, lasted several years as denial and dodging were prevalent in the face of disconfirming information, anxiety and the lack of psychological safety. He reflected that there was some overlapping of unfreezing and changing as the change process gathered momentum.

There are different levels of change and learning which have a particular relevance to action research. From the work of Bateson (1972) and others who have developed his work, a distinction between change or learning which deals with routine issues and that which involves a change of thinking or adoption of a different mental model is typically defined as a distinction between single and double loop learning (Argyris, 1982; Argyris and

Schon, 1996) and first, second or third order change (Moch and Bartunek, 1990).

First order change occurs when a specific change is identified and implemented within an existing way of thinking. For example, Bartunek et al. (1993) describe management-led action research in a bank on a problem of communication problems with clients. Through the action research process of participative data gathering, data analysis, feedback and action planning, intervention and evaluation, the named problem was addressed and improvements made.

Second order change occurs when a first order change is inadequate and the change requires lateral thinking and questioning and altering the core assumptions which underlie the situation. In another example, Bartunek et al. describe a manager-led action research project which initially aimed at addressing the improvement of a manufacturing system by increasing volume while maintaining flexibility, as well as enabling automated material control and improved planning. As the data was being analysed, it became evident that these changes would involve creating a radically new way in which the company did business. Accordingly, through the action research cycle, materials personnel, assemblers, testers and supervisors/managers participated in diagnosis, analysis and feedback resulting in the implementation of a new integrated manufacturing system. Due to the success of this project, a similar methodology was applied to other change projects in the company.

It is realized that sometimes concrete problems are symptoms of complex attitudinal and cultural problems which must be addressed and that problem resolution involves organizational transformation. This is called *third order change* which occurs when the members of an organization learn to question their own assumptions and points of view and develop and implement new ones.

Issues may not be obvious. First order problems may persist unless there is second order change. A recurrent demand for second order change may point to the need for the development of third order skills. Observation of a group at work may yield questions as to what particular behaviours or patterns of behaviour mean. What is critical is that you as the action researcher inquire into those patterns and facilitate the group in surfacing and examining them, rather than making a private interpretation which is untested and then becomes the basis for action. Taking what is directly observable into the realm of meaning requires skills in inquiry and intervention as we discussed in Chapter 3.

INTERLEVEL DYNAMICS

Levels of complexity – individual, group, inter-group, organizational – are frequently used as frameworks for understanding organizational processes. Several essential points need to be made about the concept and usage of the term levels. First, the notion of levels must be distinguished from that of echelon (Rousseau, 1985). Echelon refers to position on a chain of command in an organization, such as worker, supervisor, manager, group manager and chief executive. The less common use of organizational levels as a construct in organizational behaviour, however, describes levels of complexity.

Rashford and Coghlan (1994) present levels in terms of how people participate in organizations and link them to provide a useful tool for the manager, consultant and teacher of organizational behaviour. They distinguish four levels of behaviour in organizations – the individual, the face-to-face team, the interdepartmental group and the organization. The first level is the *bonding* relationship that the individual has with the organization and the organization with the individual. For the individual, this involves a utilization of membership and participation in the organization in order to meet personal life goals, while for management the core issue is to get a person committed to the goals, values and culture of the organization. The more complex approach to participation exists in establishing *effective working relationships in a face-to-face team*. An even more complex involvement exists in terms of the interdepartmental group type of interface where teams must be *co-ordinated* in order to achieve complex tasks and maintain a balance of power among competing political interest groups. Finally, the most complex, from the point of view of the individual, is the relationship of the total organization to its external environment in which other organizations are individual competitors, competing for scarce resources to produce similar products or services. The key task for any organization is its ability to *adapt* to environmental forces driving for change.

When you are working at each or any of the above levels, you will typically find that you are challenged to include the other levels in your diagnosis and intervention. For instance, you may be working with a team on an aspect of your action research project. In the process of this work, it emerges that some of the individual members are experiencing dissatisfaction with their relationship with the organization and do not provide optimal contribution to the team's endeavours. Or it may be that the flow of information from other teams is having a negative effect on the work of the team with which you are working. In these instances, you are challenged to move beyond the team level intervention in which you are engaged to consider dynamics at the other levels that are having an impact on the team.

Organizational levels are important dynamics in organizational politics. Organizational political behaviour may be individual, team and interdepartmental group. Individuals may engage in covert political behaviour in order to advance their own standing in the organization. Teams may engage in overt or covert political behaviour to gain advantage over others in order to obtain more resources.

Levels of analysis as described above are only one part of the picture. The other part refers to how each of the levels is related to the others. There is an essential inter-level element in that each level has a dynamic relationship with each of the others (Rashford and Coghlan, 1994). This relationship is grounded in systems dynamics, whereby the relationship each of the four levels has with the other three is systemic, with feedback loops forming a complex pattern of relationships. Dysfunctions at any of the four levels can cause dysfunctions at any of the other three levels. An individual's level of stress can be expressed in dysfunctional behaviour in the team and affect a team's ability to function effectively, which in turn affects the individual's ability to cope and ultimately the bonding relationship with the organization. If a team is not functioning effectively, it can limit the interdepartmental group's effectiveness which may depend on the quality and timeliness of information, resources and partially completed work from that team. If the interdepartmental group's multiple activities are not co-ordinated, the organization's ability to compete effectively may be affected. In systemic terms, each of the four levels affects each of the other three.

Viewing organizational levels as simply 'levels of analysis' without taking inter-level dynamics into consideration misses the point about the systemic relationship the individual has with the team, the team with the interdepartmental group, the interdepartmental group with the organization in its external environment and each with one another. There is a dynamic systemic relationship between individual bonding, team functioning, intergroup co-ordination and organizational adaptation. Understanding how interlevel dynamics between individuals, within teams and across the interdepartmental group impact the process of describing the need for change, defining the future state, assessing the present and managing the transition state is critical (Coghlan, 2000).

You may use the construct of the four levels as a diagnostic framework by being aware of the issues occurring at each level and how one level affects another, and be able to work with individuals, teams and inter-team groups to evaluate the effect of one level on another. For instance, the process of moving a change through an organization requires a systemic view of the complex interrelationship and interdependence of the individual, the face-to-face team, the interdepartmental group and the organization.

Interlevel dynamics can be seen in the case of the oil company learning history (Kleiner and Roth, 2000). In the oil company's transformational change, the CEO formed his senior managers into an executive council. The senior managers had not worked together as a team before, so it was a new experience for them to do so. They formed sub-teams to work on articulating mission, vision and values. The executive council disseminated its work to the wider organization through a learning convention.

At the convention people spoke frankly about their views of the organization for the first time and dialogue took place. The process continued through the organization, whereby the process of transforming fundamental ways of thinking and feeling moved from the CEO to the executive council through the organization and impacted teams and individuals.

Coghlan (1996) analysed the change process in his organization through the framework of organizational levels. The development of policy in order to adapt to the changing environment was analysed in conjunction with its effects on the co-ordination of units of the organization, the functioning of teams and the bonding relationship to the organization by the members. Change in the organization was initiated at the level of the organization's policy and strategy and, when that was blocked by individuals' denial of the need for change, strategic attention was focused on individual development and subsequently team development in order to create the context in which apostolic and strategic change could occur. The experience of the progress of change in the organization was analysed through the construct of the four organizational levels in order to understand what was happening in the organization at particular times and how success in progressing the change issues depended on integration of the linkages between each of the four levels.

Interlevel dynamics are also useful for understanding the action research process itself. First-person research in my own organization, how the research is for me, is linked to my own sense of bonding to the organization. As we have seen, how the research contributes to my own development, my role and future in the organization is a significant aspect of undertaking research in my own organization. Accordingly, my own self-awareness, closeness to the issues, how I frame the issues and so on are critical first-person processes of which I have to be aware and to work on consciously as part of the research project. Second-person research is particularly critical to action research as it involves building and managing the collaborative relationships within the organization to work on the project.

All four levels may be operative in second-person research. The project work with individuals may have an impact on their bonding relationship with the organization. The action research process typically involves working collaboratively at team, inter-departmental group and organizational levels. So you may seek to engage a key individual in your action research project. That individual may deny the relevance of the project or dodge becoming involved. If your persistence succeeds, then you are likely to engage a team or group in the project. The team relationships may be formal team-level relationships, informal teams or temporary ad hoc groups or committees. The team members may typically respond to your initiation by denying and dodging at the initial stages. In a similar fashion, engaging intergroup co-operation at the interdepartmental group level will involve working at interfunctional and interdepartmental co-operation. The skills in building and maintaining such collaborative relationships with individuals, teams, across teams and across organizations are critical to the success of the project.

CONCLUSIONS

In this chapter we have outlined how you would approach making sense of complex organizational data. We have presented some major themes with respect to how you might go about choosing a framework on which you would base your understanding of organizational data and on the basis of which you would take action.

Making sense has different applications in different contexts where the action research in your own organization is linked to academic accreditation. In a masters programme such as an MBA or its equivalent, frameworks such as those discussed in this chapter are used to help you see more clearly what is going on and to design appropriate interventions to deal with the issues identified.

In a masters by research and a PhD you go further. In this context, you not only use the frameworks to help you see what is going on and to plan further action, but you also critique and extend theoretical frameworks in order to contribute to theory development. Coghlan (1996) provides an example of where the story of the organization's change process contributed to understanding organizational change in terms of interlevel dynamics.

EXERCISE 8.1: DIAGNOSING YOUR ORGANIZATION

Take any organizational diagnostic framework from any text-book and apply the boxes and process lines to your own organization.

1 What picture is emerging?
2 What do you need to do to check the picture you have of the organization?
3 Where do you think you need to intervene?
4 How do you justify that diagnosis and intervention selection?

EXERCISE 8.2: USING SYSTEMS PRACTICE

Some useful books which can help you do some systems think-ing and mapping are: Anderson and Johnson (1997); Balle (1994); Senge et al. (1994). On a sheet of paper:

1 Describe the issue/problem as you see it.
2 Tell the story.
3 Draw a map of the story: When A said/did . . . What did B do? What did A do next? What was the outcome for C?
4 Connect the process of the story with arrows.
5 Include where you are in the story and what your interests are.
6 Consider any number of explanations of the patterns.
7 Consider any number of interventions which might change the structure of the system and see how each intervention has different outcomes across the system.

EXERCISE 8.3: APPLYING INTERLEVEL DYNAMICS

1 (a) Who are the individuals involved in this project? How do I work with them?
    (b) Who are the teams involved in this project? How do I work with them?
    (c) What are the issues between these teams? How do I work at the inter-team level?
2 In the teams in the project, what impact are individuals having on the team in which they are members and vice versa?
3 What are the significant patterns of relationships between individuals, teams, the interdepartmental group and the organization that I need to be sensitive to and work with?

9

Writing an Action Research Dissertation

At the end of the academic-oriented action research project you have to write a dissertation. In non-academic contexts you may write a report or want to write an article or paper. In this chapter we explore how to structure and present such a document. Our primary focus is the academic dissertation, though many of the points we make apply to the other contexts as well.

A dissertation is an academic document and therefore needs to conform to academic requirements around justification of topic and approach, description and defence of rigour in methodology and methods of inquiry, familiarity with existing content and process literature and contribution to knowledge. An action research dissertation is no different, though its presentation and argument differ from traditional presentations.

ACTION RESEARCH REPORT

There are well-established conventions on writing an action research report which are found in such action research manuals as Dick (1999), McNiff et al. (1996) and Stringer (1999). These typically suggest that the report be structured to deal with:

- purpose and rationale of the research;
- context;
- methodology and method of inquiry;
- story and outcomes;
- self-reflection and learning of the action researcher;
- reflection on the story in the light of the experience and the theory;

● extrapolation to a broader context and articulation of usable knowledge.

This is not to say that such a structure would necessarily mean that each of these headings has to be a chapter in itself, but rather that these issues be clearly dealt with formally. For example, the story may be spread over several chapters, depending on its length and complexity and the extent of the research project.

Purpose and rationale of the research

When you present the purpose and rationale of your research you are, in effect, presenting its academic context. This involves stating the reasons why what you have chosen to study is worth studying and why your actions and interventions and so on are justified. The most critical issue for you at the outset of writing an action research dissertation is to make an academic case for what you are doing. This is not just an argument for credibility but a formal effort to locate your work in an academic context.

Context

Context here refers to the social context of the research, rather than the academic context of choosing the research. In action research social context is very important. Therefore you need to describe the organization or community with which you are working. This would include details of the organization, community or group, what it does, some historical background, what its concerns are and what the issues in which you are engaging with it mean and what is intended and hoped for out of the action research project.

Methodology and method of inquiry

This is your major section on methodology in which you outline and justify your approach. Here you describe your action research approach, methodology and methods of inquiry. Methodology is your philosophical approach; methods describe what you actually did. Accordingly, you need both to articulate your methodology and your methods of inquiry.

Regarding methodology, you need to convey that you are using a normal and natural research paradigm with a long tradition and adequate rigour which is suitable for the project on which you have worked. As Dick (1999) very usefully points out, it is important to argue positively for your approach, rather than to criticize negatively the limitations of other approaches. As we presented in the earlier chapters, the action research literature provides extensive justification of how action research is scientific and rigorous.

While all research demands rigour, action research typically has to demonstrate its rigour more particularly. This is because in action research you typically start out with a fuzzy question, are fuzzy about your methodology in the initial stages and have fuzzy answers in the early stages. As the project develops your methods and answers become less fuzzy and so your questions become less fuzzy. This progression from fuzziness to clarity is the essence of the spirals of action research cycles (Gummesson, 2000). Accordingly, you need to demonstrate clearly the procedures you have used to achieve rigour and defend them. As Dick (1999) emphasizes, this means that you show:

- your use of action research learning cycles;
- how you accessed multiple data sources to provide contradictory and confirming interpretations;
- evidence of how you have challenged and tested your own assumptions and interpretations continuously throughout the project;
- how your interpretations and outcomes are challenged, supported or disconfirmed by existing literature.

Methods of inquiry refer to what we discussed in Part II and will typically focus on the content and process issues of Chapters 6 and 7. How you framed and selected the issue, built participation and support, where and how you used observation and interviews, how you engaged others in the action research cycles of implementing the project, particularly with regard to reflective learning and so on are all pertinent issues.

Story and outcomes

The heart of the dissertation is the story of what took place. At the initial stages you are likely to construct the story around a chronological narrative and structure it in terms of significant time periods or particular projects. So at the draft stages you might have narratives which cover periods of time or particular projects. This is an important structure to follow as it enables you to get the story down on paper in a logical sequence. The next stage of writing the story is to reflect on it and see what themes emerge. Then you may find that you are surfacing images or themes for the time periods or projects which capture your sense of the meaning of the project and lead you to a synthesis.

Action researchers are often surprised at what happens during the writing of a dissertation. They think that it is simply a mechanical task of writing up what is in their notes and files. Experience shows that the writing up period is a whole new learning experience. It is where synthesis and integration take place. From what have hitherto been isolated masses of details of meetings, events and organizational data, notes on scraps of paper and disks, notes from books and articles, a new reality emerges. Things begin to make sense and meanings form. For many researchers, this is the time when they realize what they have been doing all along.

Writing the story is key to synthesis. You are likely to have far more detail than you need or can use. Therefore, as you begin to select what to include and exclude, you are beginning to form a view of what is important in the story. You are at the next stage of reflective practice and indeed of action research itself. The writing project becomes an action research project as you engage in cycles of writing, reflecting, understanding how what you have written fits into the whole, and then writing further. It is far from being the mechanical task of writing up your notes.

A critical issue in presenting the story is to distinguish the events which took place, about which there is no dispute, and the meanings attributed to these events. It is important to present separately the basic story as if it were a news bulletin, as if a video camera had recorded what had taken place. This form of presentation gives the evidence in a factual and neutral manner. Your view of these events and your theorizing as to what they mean should not be mixed in with the telling of the story. This should come later, perhaps at the end of the chapter or the end of a particular phase of the story. By separating the story from its sense-making and by clearly stating which is story and which is sense-making, you are demonstrating how you are applying methodological rigour to your approach. Combining narrative and sense-making leaves you open to the charge of biased story-telling and makes it difficult for readers to evaluate your work.

In an action research dissertation sense-making often takes two forms. One is where you make sense of particular events within the narrative. It is important to do this as close to the narrative as possible. So you may have a chapter or a sequence of pages which provide a narrative of part of the story or a particular theme within it. At the end of that section you may present how you make sense of that event. You do that clearly so that the reader knows what you are doing and goes back to the story to see how your interpretations make sense. It is important that your sense-making sections are not too far from the story narrative. If you leave all your sense-making to chapters at the end, particularly in a doctoral dissertation, it makes it difficult for the reader to remember to what you are referring. The second form sense-making takes is that you have a general chapter towards the end of the dissertation which integrates the more specific interpretations you have made and provides an overview of your sense-making of the whole story.

It is at this stage that you may have to engage in a further content literature review. As you are making sense of the story you will find that you are being drawn into more specific or even new areas of content, whose literature you now need to review. In action research projects, specific relevant content areas emerge as the project progresses, so you often do not quite know what the focus of your synthesis is until the project is well in progress. Content literature becomes more focused through the story and directly relates to what is being framed in the story.

Self-reflection and learning of the action researcher

An important part of the action research dissertation is your reflection on your own learning. As you have been intervening in the organizational system over the period of the action research project, you need to articulate what you have learned, not only about the system you have been working to change, but about yourself as an action researcher. The project may have challenged many of your assumptions, attitudes, skills and existing organizational relationships.

Winter (1989) argues that your presentation should reflect your own process of learning and not be a judgement of others. He makes the relevant point that you should avoid making commentaries which place you as the researcher in the superior role of one whose analysis of other people's words show that you understand what took place, while they do not. He suggests that your commentary should place you at risk, as the single voice of the author in a context where many people participated in the work.

One particular dilemma that action researchers face in writing their reports is whether to use the personal first-person or the impersonal third-person narrative style when referring to themselves as the researcher or author. There is no consensus. Krim (1988) and Treleaven (1994) use the personal 'I' throughout; Coghlan (1996) and Goode and Bartunek (1990) refer to the impersonal 'the consultant'. A useful guideline in our experience is that if the report contains extensive reflection on the personal learning of the author researcher as agent of the action in the story (as instanced by Krim), then the first-person narrative adds a considerable strength to the published report. Third-person narrative gives a sense of objectivity, while using the first-person demands that the distinction between the story's narrative and the researcher's interpretation and sense-making be very clearly distinct.

Reflection on the story in the light of experience

One of the most common criticisms of published action research is that it lacks theory. In other words, action research accounts tell a story but do not address issues of emergent theory and so contribute to knowledge. Accordingly, your action research project needs to apply some established theory or create some new theory. The scope of the academic project, whether masters or doctorate, will be an important determinant of what is to be expected in this regard.

If you are a participant in a masters programme engaging in pragmatic action research, such as an action-oriented MBA programme, you use frameworks to make sense of what is going on. You may be drawing on frameworks which help you make sense of an industry analysis, performance of the firm and the like. Your use of these frameworks aligns the story to the theory, and through this alignment you demonstrate your understanding of the theory and its application.

If you are engaged in a more research-oriented programme, such as a masters by research or a doctorate, you are not only aligning the story with theory, but also extending that theory or developing a new one. This extension is an inductive process, coming out of your meta learning of reflecting on the implementation of the action research cycles with the members of the systems as they enact the action research project. This new theory or extension of existing theory may be in content, as instanced in Coghlan's (1996) application of interlevel dynamics to large system change in a longitudinal study, or process, as in Krim's (1988) developmental action inquiry approach to learning in a political environment.

Extrapolation to a broader context and articulation of usable knowledge

As a consequence of your reflection on the story and articulation of usable knowledge, you need to articulate how your research project can be extrapolated to a wider context. Such an extrapolation answers the 'so what?' question in relation to your research and completes the agenda that good research is for me, for us and for them; that is, it integrates first, second and third person research (Reason and Marshall, 1987). This section is answering the question: 'Why should anyone who has not been involved directly in my research be interested in it?'

Action research projects are situation specific and do not aim to create universal knowledge. At the same time, extrapolation from a local situation to more general situation is important. As an action researcher you are not claiming that every organization will behave as the one you have studied. But you can focus on some significant factors, consideration of which is useful for other organizations, perhaps similar organizations or organizations undergoing similar types of change processes.

For readers whose action research is directed at both a practical organizational outcome and an academic assessment, it may be useful for you to produce two documents. Organizational readers tend to be interested primarily in the story and its analysis and less interested in academic citations, critiques of methodology, literature reviews and discussions of theoretical differences between schools of thought, which are central to an academic dissertation. For the organizational readers, the researcher may produce a report which contains the core story and its analysis, omitting the academic requirements.

DISSEMINATION

Dissemination of action research occurs in ways similar to all forms of research dissemination. A dissertation is held in a library, with its abstract circulated on abstract indexes. Articles and papers may be submitted to journals and books. Throughout this book we have referenced many such published accounts.

Political sensitivities are typically critical issues in the writing of the research report and its dissemination. The content of the report may contain classified material or data of interest to competitors. Individual actors may be identifiable and their reported role in the events of the story may not be complimentary. Conventions relating to disguising the identity of the case and the actors may be applied. Krim (1988) does not identify the city hall in which his research took place and probably, for most readers, its identity is irrelevant and subordinate to the theme and methodology of the research.

A particular application of action research dissemination involves those who have participated as co-researchers in the project. You may have a moral obligation to involve them in the conclusions and the report. In terms of communicating your analysis back to the organization, Nielsen and Repstad (1993) advise:

- Do not promise greater anonymity than you can keep.
- Take actors' analyses seriously.
- Point to potential solutions.

● Take the opportunity to discuss with as many as possible.

> *Coghlan's (1996) research report was circulated among the then current executive and his staff and seminars were held on what the organization might have learned about the change process over time. Coghlan acted as a process consultant as the executive and his team explored how the current organization was functioning and how the planning and renewal structures could be revitalized.*
>
> *Roth and Kleiner (2000) provide a template of how a learning history may be introduced to readers. They discourage reading it as a report, but rather encourage approaching it in an inquiry mode by suspending judgement, wondering why people said what they said, and so on. They suggest discussing the case with others and that readers be prepared to think about their own perceptions and reactions to the case. The conversations about the case might be structured around: (a) what happened and why, what reactions readers have to the materials; and (b) what the implications and generalizations might be.*

CONCLUSIONS

Writing the action research dissertation is an act of learning and is itself an action research project. During the writing of the dissertation you draw together the complexities of all your data and engage in a sense-making activity that integrates your own personal learning as well as what took place in the system in which you worked. Telling the story, making sense of it, applying a rigorous methodology to that sense-making are directed toward the generation of useful knowledge which must produce outcomes which are of value to others.

A Final Word

In this book we have explored a subject which has received very little attention, and yet represents very common practice in post-experience masters and doctoral programmes of business education, health care, social work and third sector organizations.

Action research is about undertaking action and studying that action as it takes place. It is about improving practice through intervention, and demands rigorous preparation, planning, action, attention to process, reflection, replanning and validating claims to learning and theory generation. It is collaborative, involving interacting with others. We have focused on the dynamics of how this might be done when the action research is being undertaken in the organization of the action researcher, who is both aiming at achieving personal goals from the project and contributing to the organization. We drew on the image, adapted from Weisbord, of the actor-director in the act of making a movie. Movie-making involves creating a script whereby the story of the movie is enacted by people in interaction with one another over time. The actor-director engages in both acting in the movie and standing back to study how the shots are being taken, how the actors are performing and deciding how subsequent shots need to be set up.

We began our exploration by understanding the basic tenets of action research and unravelling the multiple forms it takes. Then we explored the two core foundational elements: how action research works through (a) the spirals of cycles of diagnosing, planning, taking and evaluating action, and the meta cycle of content, process and premise reflection; and (b) how the individual researcher learns in action. In all this the critical skills are introspective reflection and, when engaging with others, combining advocacy with inquiry. While many of the issues of any research project pertain to researching your own organization, the particular challenges posed by researching your own organization are around managing the closeness–distance tension, and managing the politics in order that you have a future in the organization when the research is completed.

Nielsen and Repstad (1993) describe the notion of researching your own organization in terms of a journey from nearness to distance and back and provide some practical advice. In terms of maintaining distance, they advise that you be aware of your preconceived ideas and prejudices about the organization and find rational theories to explain the organization as a way of distancing yourself. They suggest that you perform the role of devil's advocate by finding alternative theories which contradict the rational theories you have selected to explain the organization by engaging in dialogue with other members of the organization. In their view, you need to consider seriously the prevailing explanation of organizational problems, which might reflect analyses of symptoms. These would typically be (a) the scapegoat syndrome – 'who is to blame'; (b) too little information – 'if only we had more'; (c) too few resources – 'if only we had more'.

What you can do in an action research project in your own organization depends on the formal and psychological contract you have with the system on its commitment to learning in action juxtaposed with yours. This is critical to the nature of the project you can undertake. You draw on your preunderstanding of the organization and how you can manage the twin roles of your regular organizational role with the researcher role. With that foundation we explored some important and useful issues – managing organizational politics, framing and selecting a project, implementing it and, finally, writing an action research dissertation.

For some readers doing action research in their own organizations is an exciting, demanding and invigorating prospect which will contribute considerably to their own learning and help their career development. For others it may seem daunting with a high potential for self-destruction. Can you survive doing action research in your own organization? Shepard (1997) provides a few rules of thumb for change agents which are also useful for insider action researchers.

1 *Stay alive.* Care for yourself. Keep a life outside the project so as to be able to turn yourself on and off. Stay in touch with the purpose of the project and go with the flow.
2 *Start where the system is.* Have empathy with the system and the people in it, particularly as it will not like being 'diagnosed'.
3 *Never work uphill.* Keep working at collaboration and work in the most promising arena.
4 *Innovation requires a good idea, initiative and a few friends.* Find the people who are ready to work on the project and get them working together.
5 *Load experiments with success.* Work at building success steps along the way.
6 *Light many fires.* Remember the notion of systems. Any part of a system is the way it is because of how the rest of the system is. As you work towards change in one part, other parts will push the system back to the way it was. Understand the interdependencies among subsystems and keep movement going in as many of them as you can.
7 *Keep an optimistic bias.* Stay focused on vision and desired outcomes.
8 *Capture the moment.* Stay in tune with yourself and the situation.

Friedman (in press) suggests four attributes: be proactive and reflective; be critical and committed; be independent and work well with others; have aspirations and be realistic about limits. With these in mind we are confident that not only can you survive doing action research in your own organization, but you can flourish and be successful.

References

Adler, P.A. and Adler, P. (1987) *Membership Roles in Field Research*. Thousand Oaks, CA: Sage.

Aguinis, H. (1993) 'Action research and scientific method: presumed discrepancies and actual similarities', *Journal of Applied Behavioral Science*, 29 (4): 416–431.

Anderson, V. and Johnson, L. (1997) *Systems Thinking Basics: From Concepts to Causal Loops*. Cambridge, MA: Pegasus.

Argyris, C. (1982) *Reasoning, Learning and Action*. San Francisco, CA: Jossey-Bass.

Argyris, C. (1990) *Overcoming Organizational Defenses*. Boston, MA: Allyn and Bacon.

Argyris, C. (1993) *Knowledge for Action*. San Francisco, CA: Jossey-Bass.

Argyris, C. (1999) *On Organizational Learning*. Oxford: Blackwell.

Argyris, C. and Schon, D. (1996) *Organizational Learning II*. Reading, MA: Addison-Wesley.

Argyris, C., Putnam, R. and Smith, D. (1985) *Action Science*. San Francisco, CA: Jossey-Bass.

Balle, M. (1994) *Managing with Systems Thinking*. London: McGraw-Hill.

Bartunek, J.M. (1988) 'The dynamics of personal and organizational reframing', in R. Quinn and K. Cameron (eds), *Paradox and Transformation: Toward a Theory of Change in Organizations and Management*. Cambridge, MA: Ballinger. pp. 137–162.

Bartunek, J.M. and Louis, M.R. (1996) *Insider/Outsider Team Research*. Thousand Oaks, CA: Sage.

Bartunek, J.M., Crosta, T.E., Dame, R.F. and LeLacheur, D.F. (1993) 'Managers and project leaders conducting their own action research interventions', in R.T. Golembiewski (ed.), *Handbook of Organizational Consultation*. New York: Marcel Dekker. pp. 27–36.

Bartunek, J.M., Krim, R., Necochea, R. and Humphries, M. (1999) 'Sensemaking, sensegiving and leadership in strategic organization development', in J. Wagner III (ed.), *Advances in Qualitative Research*, vol. 2. Greenwich, CT: JAI. pp. 37–71.

Baskerville, R. and Wood-Harper, A.T. (1996) 'A critical perspective on action research as a method for information systems research', *Journal of Information Technology*, 11, 235–246.

Bateson, G. (1972) *Steps to an Ecology of Mind*. San Francisco, CA: Ballantine.

Bawden, R. (1991) 'Towards action research systems', in O. Zuber-Skerritt (ed.), *Action Research for Change and Development*. Aldershot: Avebury. pp. 10–35.

Beckhard, R. and Harris, R. (1987) *Organizational Transitions: Managing Complex Change*, 2nd edn. Reading, MA: Addison-Wesley.

Beckhard, R. and Pritchard, W. (1992) *Changing the Essence: The Art of Creating and Leading Fundamental Change in Organizations*. San Francisco, CA: Jossey-Bass.

Bentz, V.M. and Shapiro J.J. (1998) *Mindful Inquiry in Social Research*. Thousand Oaks, CA: Sage.

Bolman, D. and Deal, T. (1997) *Reframing Organizations*, 2nd edn. San Francisco, CA: Jossey-Bass.

Brannick, T. and Roche, W.K. (1997) *Business Research Methods: Strategies, Techniques and Sources*. Dublin: Oak Tree Press.

Brooks, A. and Watkins, K.E. (1994) *The Emerging Power of Action Inquiry Technologies*. San Francisco, CA: Jossey-Bass.

Buchanan, D. and Badham, R. (1999) *Power, Politics and Organizational Change: Winning the Turf Game*. London: Sage.

Buchanan, D. and Boddy, D. (1992) *The Expertise of the Change Agent*. London: Prentice Hall.

Burke, W.W. (1994a) *Organization Development: A Process of Learning and Changing*, 2nd edn. Reading, MA: Addison-Wesley.

Burke, W.W. (1994b) 'Diagnostic models for organization development', in A. Howard and Associates (eds), *Diagnosis for Organizational Change*. New York: Guilford. pp. 53–84.

Checkland, P. and Holwell, S. (1998) 'Action research: its nature and validity', *Systemic Practice and Action Research*, 11 (1): 9–21.

Chisholm, R.F. (1998) *Developing Network Organizations*. Reading, MA: Addison-Wesley.

Clark, P. (1972) *Action Research and Organizational Change*. London: Harper and Row.

Coch, L. and French, J.R.P. (1948) 'Overcoming resistance to change', *Human Relations*, 1: 512–532.

Coghlan, D. (1993a) 'Learning from emotions through journaling', *Journal of Management Education*, 17 (1): 90–94.

Coghlan, D. (1993b) 'A person-centred approach to dealing with resistance to change', *Leadership and Organization Development Journal*, 14 (4): 10–14.

Coghlan, D. (1994) 'Change as re-education: Lewin revisited', *Organization Development Journal*, 12 (4): 1–8.

Coghlan, D. (1996) 'Mapping the progress of change through organizational levels: the example of a religious order', in R. Woodman and W. Pasmore (eds*)*, *Research in Organizational Change and Development*, vol. 9. Greenwich, CT: JAI. pp. 123–150.

Coghlan, D. (1997) 'Organizational learning as a dynamic interlevel process', in M.A. Rahim, R.T. Golembiewski and L.E. Pate (eds), *Current Topics in Management*, vol. 2. Greenwich, CT: JAI. pp. 27–44.

Coghlan, D. (2000) 'The interlevel dynamics of large system change', *Organization Development Journal*, 18 (1): 41–50.

Coghlan, D. and McDonagh, J. (1997) 'Doing action science in your own organization', in T. Brannick and W.K. Roche, *Business Research Methods: Strategies, Techniques and Sources*. Dublin: Oak Tree Press. pp. 139–161.

Coghlan, D. and Rashford, N.S. (1990) 'Uncovering and dealing with organizational distortions', *Journal of Managerial Psychology*, 5 (3): 17–21.

Cooklin, A. (1999) 'Frameworks for the organization and for the agent of change', in A. Cooklin (ed.) *Changing Organizations: Clinicians as Agents of Change*. London: Karnac. pp. 1–26.

Cooperrider, D.L. and Srivastva, S. (1987) 'Appreciative inquiry in organizational life', in R. Woodman and W. Pasmore (eds), *Research in Organizational Change and Development*, vol. 1. Greenwich, CT: JAI. pp. 129–169.

Cooperrider, D.L., Sorensen, P.F., Whitney, D. and Yaeger, T.F. (eds) (2000) *Appreciative Inquiry: Rethinking Organization Toward a Positive Theory of Change*. Champaign, IL: Stipes.

Cunningham, J.B. (1993) *Action Research and Organization Development*. Westport, CT: Praeger.

Daudelin, M.W. (1996) 'Learning from experience through reflection', *Organizational Dynamics*, 24 (3): 36–48.

Dick, B. (1999) 'You want to do an action research thesis?' *http://www.scu.edu.au/schools/sawd/arr/arth/arthesis.html*

Dickens, L. and Watkins, K. (1999) 'Action research: rethinking Lewin', *Management Learning*, 30 (2): 127–140.

Dutton, J.E. and Duncan, R.B. (1987) 'The creation of momentum for change through the process of strategic issue diagnosis', *Strategic Management Journal*, 8: 279–295.

Dutton, J.E. and Jackson, S.E. (1987) 'Categorizing strategic issues: links to organizational action', *Academy of Management Review*, 12 (1): 76–90.

Dutton, J.E. and Ottensmeyer, E. (1987) 'Strategic issues management systems: forms, functions and contexts', *Academy of Management Review*, 12 (2): 355–365.

Dutton, J.E., Fahey, L. and Narayanan, V.K. (1983) 'Toward understanding strategic issue diagnosis', *Strategic Management Journal*, 4: 307–323.

Eden, C. and Huxham, C. (1996) 'Action research for the study of organizations', in S.R. Clegg, C. Hardy and W.R. Nord (eds), *Handbook of Organization Studies*. Thousand Oaks, CA: Sage. pp. 526–542.

Elden, M. and Chisholm, R.F. (1993) 'Emerging varieties of action research: introduction to the special issue', *Human Relations*, 46 (2): 121–141.

Elizur, Y. (1999) '"Inside" consultation through self-differentiation: stimulating organization development in the IDF's care of intractable, war-related, traumatic disorders', in A. Cooklin (ed.) *Changing Organizations: Clinicians as Agents of Change*. London: Karnac. pp. 141–168.

Elliot, J. (1991) *Action Research for Educational Change*. Milton Keynes: Open University Press.

Evans, M. (1997) 'An action research enquiry into reflection in action as part of my role as a deputy headteacher'. PhD thesis, Kingston University. *http://www.bath.ac.uk/~edsajw/moyra.html*

Evered, M. and Louis, M.R. (1981) 'Alternative perspectives in the organizational sciences: "inquiry from the inside" and "inquiry from the outside"', *Academy of Management Review,* 6, 385–395.

Fals-Borda, O. and Rahman, M. (1991) *Action and Knowledge.* New York: Apex Press.

Fisher, D. and Torbert, W.R. (1995) *Personal and Organizational Transformations.* New York: McGraw-Hill.

Fisher, R. and Ury, W. (1986) *Getting to Yes.* London: Business Books.

Foster, M. (1972) 'An introduction to the theory and practice of action research in work organizations', *Human Relations,* 25 (6): 529–556.

French, W. and Bell, C. (1999) *Organization Development: Behavioral Science Interventions for Organization Improvement,* 6th edn. Englewood Cliffs, NJ: Prentice Hall.

Friedman, V. (in press) 'The individual as agent of organizational learning', in M. Dierkes, J. Child, I. Nonaka and A. Berthoin Antal (eds), *Handbook of Organizational Learning.* Oxford: Oxford University Press.

Friedman, V. and Lipshitz, R. (1992) 'Teaching people to shift cognitive gears: overcoming resistance on the road to model II', *Journal of Applied Behavioral Science,* 28 (1): 118–136.

Frohman, A.L. (1997) 'Igniting organizational change from below: the power of personal initiative', *Organizational Dynamics,* winter: 39–53.

Frohman, M., Sashkin, M. and Kavanagh, M. (1976) 'Action research as applied to organization development', *Organization and Administrative Sciences,* 7 (1) and (2): 129–142.

Golembiewski, R.T. and Varney, G. (1999) *Cases in Organization Development.* Itasca, IL: F.E. Peacock.

Goode, L.M. and Bartunek, J.M. (1990) 'Action research in an underbounded setting', *Consultation,* 9 (3): 209–228.

Gosling, J. and Ashton, D. (1994) 'Action learning and academic qualifications', *Management Learning,* 25 (2): 263–274.

Greenwood, D. and Levin, M. (1998) *Introduction to Action Research.* Thousand Oaks, CA: Sage.

Greiner, L.E. and Schein, V.E. (1988) *Power and Organization Development.* Reading, MA: Addison-Wesley.

Gummesson, E. (2000) *Qualitative Methods in Management Research,* 2nd edn. Thousand Oaks, CA: Sage.

Hammond, S.A. and Royal, C. (1998) *Lessons from the Field: Applying Appreciative Inquiry.* Plano, TX: Practical Press.

Hanna, D. (1987) *Designing Organizations for High Performance.* Reading, MA: Addison-Wesley.

Harrison, M. and Shirom, A. (1999) *Organizational Diagnosis and Assessment: Bridging Theory and Practice.* Thousand Oaks, CA: Sage.

Hart, E. and Bond, M. (1995) *Action Research for Health and Social Care: A Guide to Practice.* Milton Keynes: Open University Press.

Heron, J. (1988) 'Validity in cooperative inquiry', in P. Reason, *Human Inquiry in Action.* London: Sage. pp. 40–59.

Heron, J. (1996) *Co-operative Inquiry.* London: Sage.

Heron, J. and Reason, P. (1997) 'A participatory inquiry paradigm', *Qualitative Inquiry*, 33: 274–294.

Hill, M.R. (1993) *Archival Strategies and Techniques*. Thousand Oaks, CA: Sage.

Holian, R. (1999) 'Doing action research in my own organization: ethical dilemmas, hopes and triumphs', *Action Research International*, Paper 3. *http://www.scu.edu.au/schools/sawd/ari/ari/holian.html*

Holley, E. (1997) 'How do I as a teacher-researcher contribute to the development of a living educational theory through an exploration of my values in my professional practice?' M.Phil thesis, University of Bath.
http://www.bath.ac.uk/-edsajw/erica.html

Holter, I. and Schwartz-Barcott, D. (1993) 'Action research: what is it, how has it been used and how can it be used in nursing?', *Journal of Advanced Nursing*, 18 (2): 298–304.

Homa, P. (1998) 'Re-engineering the Leicester Royal Infirmary healthcare process'. Unpublished PhD thesis, Henley Management College and Brunel University.

Kakabadse, A. (1984) 'Politics of a process consultant', in A. Kakabadse and C. Parker (eds), *Power, Politics and Organizations*. Chichester: Wiley. pp. 169–183.

Katz, D. and Kahn, R.L. (1978) *The Social Psychology of Organizations*, 2nd edn. New York: McGraw-Hill.

Kemmis, S. and McTaggart, R. (eds) (1988) *The Action Research Planner*. Victoria: Deakin University Press.

Kleiner, A. and Roth, G. (1997) 'How to make experience your company's best teacher', *Harvard Business Review*, September–October: 172–177.

Kleiner, A. and Roth, G. (2000) *Oil Change*. New York: Oxford University Press.

Kolb, D. (1984) *Experiential Learning*. Englewood Cliffs, NJ: Prentice Hall.

Kotter, J. (1985) *Power and Influence: Beyond Formal Authority*. New York: Free Press.

Krim, R. (1988) 'Managing to learn: action inquiry in city hall', in P. Reason, *Human Inquiry in Action*. London: pp. 144–162.

Lanzara, G.F. (1991) 'Shifting stones: learning from a reflective experiment in a decision process', in D.A. Schon (ed.), *The Reflective Turn*. New York: Teachers College, Columbia University. pp. 285–320.

Lewin, K. (1966) 'Group decision and social change', in E. Maccoby, T. Newcomb and E. Hartley (eds), *Readings in Social Psychology*, 2nd edn. New York: Holt, Rinehart and Winston. pp. 197–211.

Lewin, K. (1973) 'Action research and minority problems', in K. Lewin, *Resolving Social Conflicts: Selected Papers on Group Dynamics* (ed. G. Lewin). London: Souvenir Press. pp. 201–216.

Lippitt, R. (1979) 'Kurt Lewin, action research and planned change', paper provided by the author.

Lynch, K. (1999) 'Equality studies, the academy and the role of research in emancipatory social change', *Economic and Social Review*, 30 (1): 41–69.

McCaughan, N. and Palmer, B. (1994) *Systems Thinking for Harassed Managers*. London: Karnac.

McGill, I. and Beaty, L. (1995) *Action Learning*, 2nd edn. London: Kogan Page.

McMullan, W. and Cahoon, A. (1979) 'Integrating abstract conceptualizing with experiential learning', *Academy of Management Review*, 4 (3): 453–458.

McNiff, J., Lomax, P. and Whitehead, J. (1996) *You and Your Action Research Project*. London: Routledge.

Marquardt, M.J. (1999) *Action Learning in Action*. Palo Alto, CA: Davies-Black.

Marrow, A.J (1969) *The Practical Theorist*. New York: Basic Books.

Marshall, J. (1995) *Women Managers Moving On*. London: Routledge.

Marshall, J. and Reason, P. (1993) 'Adult learning in collaborative action research: reflections on the supervision process', *Studies in Continuing Education*, 15 (2): 117–132.

Mellish, L. (1998) 'Strategic planning: appreciative inquiry in a large-scale change at an Australian university', in S.A. Hammond and C. Royal (eds), *Lessons from the Field: Applying Appreciative Inquiry*. Plano, TX: Practical Press. pp. 49–61.

Mezirow, J. (1991) *Transformative Dimensions of Adult Learning*. San Francisco, CA: Jossey-Bass.

Miller, N. (1994) 'Participatory action research: principles, politics and possibilities', in A. Brooks and K.E. Watkins, *The Emerging Power of Action Inquiry Technologies*. San Francisco, CA: Jossey-Bass.

Moch, M.K. and Bartunek, J.M. (1990) *Creating Alternative Realities at Work*. New York: Harper.

Nielsen, J.C.R. and Repstad, P. (1993) 'From nearness to distance – and back: analyzing your own organization'. Copenhagen Business School, Institute of Organizational and Industrial Sociology, Papers in Organizations no. 14.

Nuttall, P.A. (1998) 'Understanding "empowerment": a study in a manufacturing company'. Unpublished PhD Thesis, Henley Management College and Brunel University.

Pace, L.A. and Argona, D.R. (1991) 'Participatory action research: a view from Xerox', in W.W. Whyte (ed.), *Participatory Action Research*. Thousand Oaks, CA: Sage. pp. 56–69.

Perry, C. and Zuber-Skerritt, O. (1994) 'Doctorates by action research for senior practising managers', *Management Learning*, 25 (2): 341–364.

Pettigrew, A. (ed.) (1987) *The Management of Strategic Change*. Oxford: Blackwell.

Preskill, H. and Torres, R.T. (1999) *Evaluative Inquiry for Learning in Organizations*. Thousand Oaks, CA: Sage.

Punch M. (1994) 'Politics and ethics in qualitative research', in N. K. Denzin and Y.S. Lincoln, *Handbook of Qualitative Research*. Thousand Oaks, CA: Sage. pp. 83–97.

Putnam, R. (1991) 'Recipes and reflective learning', in D. Schon, *The Reflective Turn: Case Studies in and on Educational Practice*. New York: Teachers' College of Columbia Press. pp. 145–163.

Quigley, B.A. and Kuhne, G.W. (eds) (1997) *Creating Practical Knowledge through Action Research*. San Francisco, CA: Jossey-Bass.

Quinlan, D.R. (1996) 'Towards a re-construction of a clinical psychologist and reflexive body of practice'. Unpublished PhD thesis, University of Bath.

Raelin, J.A. (1997) 'Action learning and action science: are they different?', *Organizational Dynamics*, 26 (1): 21–34.

Raelin, J.A (1999) 'Preface', *Management Learning*, 30 (2): 115–125.

Raelin, J.A. (2000) *Work-Based Learning: The New Frontier of Management Development*. Upper Saddle, NJ: Prentice Hall.

Ramirez, I. and Bartunek, J.M. (1989) 'The multiple realities and experience of internal organization development consultation in health care', *Journal of Organizational Change Management*, 2 (1): 40–56.

Rashford, N.S. and Coghlan, D. (1994) *The Dynamics of Organizational Levels: A Change Framework for Managers and Consultants*. Reading, MA: Addison-Wesley.

Reason, P. (1988) *Human Inquiry in Action*. London: Sage.

Reason, P. (1994a) *Participation in Human Inquiry*. London: Sage.

Reason, P. (1994b) 'Three approaches to participative inquiry', in N. Denzin and Y. Lincoln (eds), *Handbook of Qualitative Research*. Thousand Oaks, CA: Sage. pp. 324–339.

Reason, P. (1999) 'Integrating action and reflection through cooperative inquiry', *Management Learning*, 30 (2): 207–226.

Reason, P. and Bradbury, H. (2000) *Handbook of Action Research*. Thousand Oaks, CA: Sage.

Reason, P. and Marshall, J. (1987) 'Research as personal process', in D. Boud and V. Griffin (eds), *Appreciating Adult Learning*, London: Kogan Page. pp. 112–126.

Reason, P. and Rowan, J. (1981) *Human Inquiry: A Sourcebook of New Paradigm Research*. Chichester: Wiley.

Reddy, W.B. (1994) *Intervention Skills: Process Consultation for Small Groups and Teams*. San Diego, CA: Pfeiffer.

Revans, R. (1998) *ABC of Action Learning*. London: Lemos and Crane.

Riemer, J. (1977) 'Varieties of opportunistic research', *Urban Life*, 5 (4): 467–477.

Rigano, D. and Edwards, J. (1998) 'Incorporating reflection into work practice: a case study', *Management Learning*, 29 (4): 431–446.

Riordan, P. (1995) 'The philosophy of action science', *Journal of Managerial Psychology*, 10 (6): 6–13. .

Ross, R. (1994) 'The ladder of inference', in P. Senge, C. Roberts, R. Ross, B. Smith and A. Kleiner (eds), *The Fifth Discipline Fieldbook*. London: Nicholas Brealey. pp. 242–246.

Ross, R. and Roberts, C. (1994) 'Balancing inquiry and advocacy', in P. Senge, C. Roberts, R. Ross, B. Smith and A. Kleiner (eds), *The Fifth Discipline Fieldbook*. London: Nicholas Brealey. pp. 253–259.

Roth, G. and Kleiner, A. (1998) 'Developing organizational memory through learning histories', *Organizational Dynamics*, 27 (3): 43–60.

Roth, G. and Kleiner, A. (2000) *Car Launch*. New York: Oxford University Press.

Rothwell, W., Sullivan, R. and McLean, G. (1995) *Practicing Organization Development*. San Diego, CA: Pfeiffer.

Rousseau, D. (1985) 'Issues in organizational research: multi-level and cross-level perspectives', in L.L. Cummings and B.M. Staw (eds), *Research in Organizational Behavior*, vol. 7. Greenwich, CT: JAI. pp. 1–37.

Rowan, J. (1981) 'A dialectical paradigm for research', in P. Reason and J. Rowan, *Human Inquiry: A Sourcebook of New Paradigm Research.* Chichester: Wiley. pp. 93–112.

Schein, E.H. (1987) *The Clinical Perspective in Fieldwork.* Newbury Park, CA: Sage.

Schein, E.H. (1992) *Organizational Culture and Leadership,* 2nd edn. San Francisco, CA: Jossey-Bass.

Schein, E.H. (1993) 'Legitimizing clinical research in the study of organizational culture', *Journal of Counseling and Development,* 71: 703–708.

Schein, E.H. (1995) 'Process consultation, action research and clinical inquiry: are they the same?', *Journal of Managerial Psychology,* 10 (6): 14–19.

Schein, E.H. (1996a) 'Three cultures of management', *Sloan Management Review,* 37 (3): 9–20.

Schein, E.H. (1996b) 'Kurt Lewin's change theory in the field and in the classroom: notes toward a model of managed learning', *Systems Practice,* 9 (1): 27–48.

Schein, E.H. (1997) 'Organizational learning: what is new?', in M.A. Rahim, R.T. Golembiewski and L.E. Pate (eds), *Current Topics in Management,* vol. 2. Greenwich, CT: JAI. pp. 11–25.

Schein, E.H. (1999a) *Process Consultation Revisited: Building the Helping Relationship.* Reading, MA: Addison-Wesley.

Schein, E.H. (1999b) *The Corporate Culture Survival Guide.* San Francisco, CA: Jossey-Bass.

Schon, D. (1983) *The Reflective Practitioner.* New York: Basic Books.

Schon, D. (1987) *Educating the Reflective Practitioner.* San Francisco, CA: Jossey-Bass.

Schon, D. (1991) *The Reflective Turn: Case Studies in and on Educational Practice.* New York: Teachers' College of Columbia Press.

Senge, P. (1990) *The Fifth Discipline.* New York: Doubleday.

Senge, P., Roberts, C., Ross, R., Smyth, B. and Kleiner, A. (1994) *The Fifth Discipline Fieldbook.* London: Nicholas Brealey.

Shepard, H. (1997) 'Rules of thumb for change agents', in D. Van Eynde, J. Hoy and D. C. Van Eynde (eds), *Organization Development Classics.* San Francisco, CA: Jossey-Bass.

Stringer, E.T. (1999) *Action Research: A Handbook for Practitioners,* 2nd edn. Thousand Oaks, CA: Sage.

Susman G. and Evered, R. (1978) 'An assessment of the scientific merits of action research', *Administrative Science Quarterly,* 23: 582–603.

Torbert, W.R. (1981) 'Why educational research has been so uneducational: the case for a new model of social science based on collaborative inquiry', in P. Reason and J. Rowan, *Human Inquiry: A Sourcebook of New Paradigm Research.* Chichester: Wiley. pp. 141–152.

Torbert, W.R. (1987) *Managing the Corporate Dream.* Homewood, IL: Dow Jones-Irwin.

Torbert, W.R. (1989) 'Leading organizational transformation', in R. Woodman and W. Pasmore (eds), *Research in Organizational Change and Development,* vol. 3. Greenwich, CT: JAI. pp. 83–116.

Torbert, W.R. (1991) *The Power of Balance.* Thousand Oaks, CA: Sage.

Torbert, W.R. (1998) 'Developing wisdom and courage in organizing and sciencing', in S. Srivastva and D. Cooperrider (eds), *Organizational Wisdom and Executive Courage*. San Francisco,CA: New Lexington Press. pp. 222–253.

Torbert, W.R. (1999) 'Distinctive questions developmental action inquiry asks', *Management Learning*, 30 (2): 189–206.

Towell, D. and Harries, C. (1978) *Innovations in Patient Care: An Action Research Study of Change in a Psychiatric Hospital*. London: Croom Helm.

Treleaven, L. (1994) 'Making a space: a collaborative inquiry with women as staff development', in P. Reason, *Participation in Human Inquiry*. London: Sage. pp. 138–162.

Ury, W. (1991) *Getting Past No*. London: Business Books.

Webb, C. (1989) 'Action research: philosophy, methods and personal experiences', *Journal of Advanced Nursing*, 14 (5): 403–410.

Weidner, K. (1999) 'It's ten o'clock. Do you know where your sponsors are? Securing and sustaining sponsorship for organizational change', *Organization Development Journal*, 17 (1): 85–94.

Weinstein, K. (1999) *Action Learning: A Practical Guide*, 2nd edn. Aldershot: Gower.

Weisbord, M.R. (1987) *Productive Workplaces*. San Francisco, CA: Jossey-Bass.

Weisbord, M.R. (1988) 'Towards a new practice theory of OD: notes on snapshooting and moviemaking', in W.A. Pasmore and R.W. Woodman (eds), *Research in Organizational Change and Development*, vol. 2. Greenwich, CT: JAI. pp. 59–96.

Wheelan, S.A. (1999) *Creating Effective Teams*. Thousand Oaks, CA: Sage.

Whyte, W.W. (ed.) (1991) *Participatory Action Research*. Thousand Oaks, CA: Sage.

Winter, R. (1989) *Learning from Experience: Principle and Practice in Action Research*. London: Falmer Press.

Young, M. (1991) *An Inside Job*. Oxford: Clarendon Press.

Name Index

Subject Index